The Servile Wars

A Captivating Guide to the Three Slave Revolts Against the Roman Republic

© Copyright 2021

All Rights Reserved. No part of this book may be reproduced in any form without permission in writing from the author. Reviewers may quote brief passages in reviews.

Disclaimer: No part of this publication may be reproduced or transmitted in any form or by any means, mechanical or electronic, including photocopying or recording, or by any information storage and retrieval system, or transmitted by email without permission in writing from the publisher.

While all attempts have been made to verify the information provided in this publication, neither the author nor the publisher assumes any responsibility for errors, omissions or contrary interpretations of the subject matter herein.

This book is for entertainment purposes only. The views expressed are those of the author alone, and should not be taken as expert instruction or commands. The reader is responsible for his or her own actions.

Adherence to all applicable laws and regulations, including international, federal, state and local laws governing professional licensing, business practices, advertising and all other aspects of doing business in the US, Canada, UK or any other jurisdiction is the sole responsibility of the purchaser or reader.

Neither the author nor the publisher assumes any responsibility or liability whatsoever on the behalf of the purchaser or reader of these materials. Any perceived slight of any individual or organization is purely unintentional.

Free Bonus from Captivating History (Available for a Limited time)

Hi History Lovers!

Now you have a chance to join our exclusive history list so you can get your first history ebook for free as well as discounts and a potential to get more history books for free! Simply visit the link below to join.

Captivatinghistory.com/ebook

Also, make sure to follow us on Facebook, Twitter and Youtube by searching for Captivating History.

Contents

INTRODUCTION 1
CHAPTER 1 – SLAVERY IN ROME 6
CHAPTER 2 – THE FOUNDATIONS OF REBELLION (OR A BRIEF HISTORY OF THE ISLAND OF SICILY) 12
CHAPTER 3 – EUNUS AND HIS PROPHECY 17
CHAPTER 4 – THE FIRST SERVILE WAR 21
CHAPTER 5 – THE CIMBRIAN WAR: CATALYST FOR THE SECOND SERVILE WAR 30
CHAPTER 6 – THE ROMANS NEED AN ARMY 35
CHAPTER 7 – THE SECOND SERVILE WAR 44
CHAPTER 8 – GLADIATORS AND THEIR LIVES 55
CHAPTER 9 – THE GLADIATORS WHO WOULD SHAKE ROME 64
CHAPTER 10 – THE THIRD SERVILE WAR 69
CONCLUSION 84
HERE'S ANOTHER BOOK BY CAPTIVATING HISTORY THAT YOU MIGHT LIKE 88
FREE BONUS FROM CAPTIVATING HISTORY (AVAILABLE FOR A LIMITED TIME) 89
REFERENCES 90

Introduction

Ancient republics were formed on the philosophies of politicians and great minds while also being built on the backs of human exploitation. For centuries, every great empire or kingdom was (and still is) divided between the powerful elite and the working class. But even with that division, there was still one class that sat below them all—slaves. Those poor individuals who found themselves at the bottom of the ladder were forced to do the jobs no one else wanted. In some ways, you may say that these empires might not have risen to such heights if it had not been for the sweat, blood, and tears of the slaves.

If one started with the first recorded evidence of slavery, they would have to follow history all the way back to ancient Sumer. It is here that archaeologists found the first mentions of laws pertaining to slaves. There, slavery existed all the way back to 2100 BCE. It seems that any empire that was built by conquering small tribes and other nations found these conquered people to be ideal for certain forms of labor. Once a tribe had been conquered, the king would sort through those remaining and choose the ones who looked the strongest, leaving the unwanted to starve and die. The ones who were chosen then were allocated to certain jobs and spent the remainder of their days serving their new masters.

No matter what region of the world an empire was in, whether the Middle East, Africa, or even the Far East, slavery became not only a necessity but also a lucrative business. However, each individual empire had different parameters and guidelines when it came to the treatment and value of slaves. Regardless, it would take a major upheaval to make any form of change.

But one thing was for sure: slavery was a booming industry and something that most either had no problem with or overlooked as if it was an everyday necessity of the time. Whether these slaves were captured in war, stolen and sold by pirates, or created through debts of their own making, there were select individuals within the populace that were nothing more than pieces of property and often treated worse than beasts of burden.

In ancient Rome, there was a large population that had found themselves being used as slave labor in all levels of society. Though there were benevolent slave owners, most slaves found their state of being to be unbearable. Eventually, like with any other empire, these less fortunate individuals would find the courage to stand up against their overlords, the Roman Republic, to win their freedom.

These wars, known as the Servile Wars, would span several decades and hundreds of miles, but none of them would quite meet the expectations of the slaves who ignited the fire of rebellion. No one in the Roman Republic would have expected that the island of Sicily would be such a hotbed for rebellion and inspire men and women to put their lives on the line for a taste of freedom. The Servile Wars were all led by charismatic and idealistic individuals who saw the pain and desire of their fellow slaves and acted upon them. Though some would eventually fall prey to that age-old corruptor of power, they would leave a mark on history.

Before diving into the historical tales, though, you have to be aware of the impact of the storytellers. There is no clear record of any of the Servile Wars, which means that the history of the wars has been told by those that either weren't there or were not part of the conflict.

Though the Servile Wars left their mark on the people of that time, each of the three slave revolts made an impression on historians (both of the time and for centuries to come). The names of the heroes and villains of these stories may be the same, though; it depends on what account you are reading. For instance, if you read Diodorus of Sicily's rendition of either of the first two Servile Wars, the Sicilian slave leaders are the heroes, and the Romans are the villains. However, a Roman historian would tell a tale where the mighty Roman legions rode in to restore order to the lawless island. And the battle locations might mirror each other, but not all of the facts are so clean-cut. Depending on the historian, Spartacus could have started with four thousand or forty thousand men.

The discrepancies are due to the political leanings and nationalities of the author. So, even though these slave rebellions played a part in changing history forever, the epic tales of the battles may well be a bit skewed. In order to piece together the happenings of these wars, we have looked at multiple sources. For the first two Servile Wars, we have turned to the books of both Titus Livius (otherwise known as Livy) and Diodorus of Sicily. Both of these works, though classics in their own times, were written well after all of the slave revolts. Through the centuries, these works have been lost to wars and devastating catastrophes, so most of the tales of these heroes and villains are fragmented at best. The wars had also been altered by the decades-long game of telephone that must have gone on before the history was put down on paper.

One of the primary sources available for the Servile Wars is the *Ab Urbe Condita Libri* ("History of Rome") by Livy. This book was written between 27 BE and 9 BCE, well after the wars had ended. Thus, Livy had to depend on records and stories from people who had been told the stories by people who had heard the stories from their elders. This, of course, questions the validity of all the information in the book.

Another source that is widely used when studying these rebellions is the *Bibliotheca Historica* ("Historical Library"), written by Diodorus Siculus (Diodorus of Sicily), a Greek historian. Diodorus's book was written sometime in the 50s BCE. In order to create his text, the historian traveled the lands, gathering accounts of the historical events of each region. He also studied in Rome's archives and took note of early Roman historians' works.

The last of the most commonly studied works when it comes to the history of the Servile Wars, particularly the third and final one, is a book written by the famous Greek biographer Plutarch. In his book, *Parallel Lives* (also known as *Lives of the Noble Greeks and Romans*), he writes a compelling biography of Crassus, the man who would defeat Spartacus. The book itself is a compilation of biographies set in groups of two men, whom Plutarch compares by their virtues. Crassus was paired with the Greek Nicias (a politician with some power during the Peloponnesian War). But because of this, the biography tends to be skewed in favor of Crassus. The book was also written in the 2nd century CE, so the facts had long been manipulated, with important pieces of information being lost, no doubt, to time.

So, you can see that though historians set about to make a definitive timeline of events, they had to use information that had been altered or had huge holes. That being said, it is possible to get a basic idea of the timeline by comparing all three sources and other historical works. To make the events come to life in this book, we have decided not to stick every assumption into these pages. But even though some of the facts are uncertain, the wars were filled with heroic deeds and courageous leaders.

The Servile Wars were filled with daring military maneuverers and devastating defeats. The men and generals that fought in them would find their names forever etched in the annals of time. Some would be immortalized as heroic figures who stood up for their fellow men, and others would be villainized for their presumption that slaves could possibly be on the same level as Roman citizens. Even though the history books may not be wholly accurate, these uprisings caused the wheels of change to begin turning in the mighty Roman Republic and the future Roman Empire.

Chapter 1 – Slavery in Rome

Understanding the atmosphere that bred the three uprisings means diving deep into slavery and the world of the Roman Republic. The Roman Republic spread over most of Europe, and in order to be able to maintain this growth, a large majority of the population was relegated to slave labor. These individuals had no dominion over themselves and were used in a wide range of industries and jobs. From simple household chores to working in the mines, these men and women (and children too) were used to ensure that those tasks that were too manually intensive and undesirable for Roman citizens got done.

Though, in our modern world, slavery is frowned upon, it was a natural and everyday occurrence that most Romans believed to be a necessity. Not only was this accepted as a societal norm, but it was also a religious and philosophical one as well. The concept of slavery and complete control over an individual was present in Roman mythology and Roman philosophy, both of which also stressed the inability for freedom without some sort of indentured servitude. As the Roman Republic expanded and more and more principalities and countries fell to them, many of the conquered populations became slaves.

Of course, not everyone was fit to become a slave. Those who had no skill to work manual labor jobs found themselves at the end of a sword. With 20 percent of the Roman Republic populace being slaves (this number, of course, ebbed and flowed with the expansion of the republic), one may wonder how the number got so high. As the republic expanded and wars were fought and won, many of the fallen enemies of the republic were taken captive and eventually sold into slavery. Not only soldiers were drafted into slavery. Those of lower social standing who had no skills to offer were also targeted. These types of slaves wound up being moved from the area they were taken to different parts of the country or even sent abroad on slave vessels to be sold in other markets.

But along with this, there was also piracy, as well as debt collection and condemnation for a crime. Civil offenses like theft would be heard during a private trial, and it was possible that the person convicted of the crime could be forced into servitude until the value of the goods that had been stolen was repaid. For those who committed a grave civil offense, they could actually end up in a life of slavery.

For those individuals who found themselves living as slaves, the desire to have a family didn't subside. Those individuals would inevitably find themselves with children, and these children were thus born into slavery.

Because of the expansion of the Roman Republic, those of noble status or who had immense lands found the need for more laborers. The influx of slaves from these regions, as well as from other means, had a huge impact on the economy, as they left the economy dependent on slavery. No matter what large city one went to in the Roman Republic, there was no doubt they would find a large slave market where men, women, and children were bought and sold like cattle. Many ports along the Mediterranean were more known for their slave markets than their actual markets.

A large number of slaves came to the shores of Italy through these markets, where they were purchased by the Roman elites. To fill these markets up, many slave traders would follow in the wake of the Roman military forces and acquire people to sell. The slave traders looked for strong men and sometimes children who could grow into strong men. Then they would take them back and sell them via public auctions or even individually to elite buyers.

The slave traders would place these slaves on display for sale in several ways. Some traders did this by putting people on revolving stages, where the slaves would have a sign around their neck with several important attributes, including where they were from and their education. The price of the slave would be determined via their age, their quality, and skills. In order to ensure that the buyers were aware of what they were buying, these slaves were put on display without any clothes. This process was overseen by low-level Roman officials.

After a while, it was clear that the influx of slaves both from the Roman conquests as well as the plethora of other sources could be beneficial to the government. This led to an eventual sales tax being placed on slaves. It originally started at 2 percent under the rule of Augustus, and eventually, by 43 CE, it worked its way up to 4 percent.

Because of the common feelings among society when it came to slaves, these poor individuals found themselves at the bottom of the barrel, with even criminals being more a citizen of the republic than them. This fact alone shows how little thought was given to the treatment and legal status of slaves in the Roman Republic.

There were many concepts and philosophies being formed during this important period in history. One of the most common was that the role of an individual was synonymous with who they were. This translated into most Roman citizens believing that a slave was not a person at all. After all, these slaves were not owners of their own bodies, lacked ancestral lineage, and tended to have no name.

This also translated into a lot of different laws being put in place in regard to slaves. For instance, a slave could not testify in any court case unless there had been bodily harm done to them by the individual. In fact, Roman slaves had very little rights whatsoever for most of the year and found themselves doing the jobs that the Roman elite couldn't be bothered with. However, the slaves could enjoy the festival of Saturnalia, which was the one day of the year where they were permitted to set down their tools and join their masters in celebration. But the next day, no matter what condition they were in, it was back to work for them.

Many slaves found themselves working multiple different jobs throughout the year, depending on the season. It was very common for a slave to work in the fields during harvest season and then to find themselves in the servitude of private homes for the remainder of the year. The main five divisions of jobs that slaves were acquired to do were domestic, public, urban works and services, farming, and mining. Their jobs would be further broken down into specific work within these fields.

How the slaves lived would depend on what type of job they were purchased to do. For those who were brought into a Roman elite's or noble's home, their living spaces were often much more comfortable and elaborate than those who lived in a tradesman's home. Though they didn't have a comfortable life by any stretch of the imagination, many of the Roman elite household slaves had their own quarters and modest clothing. After all, the number of slaves a person had was a sign of their standing in society, and being able to clothe and house numerous slaves would reflect well on them.

On the other hand, those who were chosen to work in the mines and quarries lived out their days doing strenuous manual labor and living in hovels. If a person wound up being purchased by a gladiator school or a nobleman who wanted his own gladiator, they would have a unique life that could possibly be both full of fame and torture. Another form of employment that was open to slaves was that of a servus publicus. These slaves were not privately owned but were rather owned by the public in general. Most of these slaves wound up doing work in temples and colleges. This gave them a unique life, just like the slaves who found their way into gladiator schools. Many of these slaves would gain some education, and that would give them a pretty big advantage when it came to possibly gaining their freedom. There were even some slaves who were able to build a reputation for themselves and do more skilled work, as well as earn money. Many times, this type of slave could work their way into manumission more easily than other slaves.

The intensive labor that the slaves of the Roman Republic endured was backbreaking and exhausting, but there was the ability for some slaves to claim freedom. Manumission, in essence, means that slaves were either freed by their owners or had worked off their debt, thereby earning their freedom. Unlike Greece, Rome treated freed slaves in a much more compassionate manner. After manumission (the act of a master freeing a slave), these men and women could work their way into becoming a citizen of the republic. Manumission was done in full view of the public and was overseen by a public official to make it legal. The master looking to release the slave would use a staff and touch it to the slave's head to proclaim the slave's freedom. After this ceremony had been performed, the slave was then given a felt cap to wear as a sign that they had been freed.

Manumission allowed slaves the opportunity to own property, as well as to participate in government, that is, as long as they were born a male. These former slaves fell into the social class known as the libertini. Although they could vote and accumulate wealth, they were unable to run for any office. Still, freed slaves had the ability to gain influence even without having any type of official power.

The process of building one's reputation was lengthy and included a period of time where their previous master became their patron. The arrangement left the master and now freed slave with a list of obligations that had to be completed before the slave was truly free.

Along with this, any child born after a slave had been freed would be born a citizen with full rights. The process of manumission was very difficult and very rare, but there are documents and stories about slaves who were able to do this. However, for the majority of slaves, this was not an option.

Roman masters saw their slaves as nothing more than property, and this left them with the ability to treat their slaves as they saw fit. That meant that many slaves lived in squalor and harsh environments, which broke not only their bodies but also their spirits. Living in this fashion ravaged many and led to numerous deaths. However, it would also lead to several individuals standing up from the crowd and inspiring their fellow slaves to stand with them. These leaders of the beaten-down masses of the slave class would look to make some impact on the world they lived in. The first of these individuals would ignite a fire on the island of Sicily in 135 BCE.

Chapter 2 – The Foundations of Rebellion (Or a Brief History of the Island of Sicily)

Pressure had been building for decades on the little island of Sicily. Rebellions like the ones that made up the first two Servile Wars weren't just born; they were cultivated, and they started in 900 BCE. The native Sicilians, who consisted of multiple small tribes, had been trading with the mighty Phoenician Empire for quite some time. Eventually, the Phoenicians decided it would be best to set up trading posts to cement their partnership with these native tribes. It also had the added benefit of making their presence felt at all times. Not needing to go much farther inland than the coast, the Phoenicians left a majority of the island open for other nations to settle. This would be one of the many catalysts that left the island ripe for rebellion in 135 BCE.

In 750 BCE, the first of these other nations would land when Greek ships sailed into the harbors on the western side of the island. For centuries, this division of the island seemed to work just fine, but eventually, the Phoenician posts would be enveloped into the Carthaginian hegemony. As the Greeks continued expanding throughout the Mediterranean, the Magonid dynasty stepped up to stop that expansion, and the Carthaginian hegemony was born. This union would be the spark that ignited several flames of rebellion, which would lead to centuries of dissent and bloody battles. In regards to Sicily, the Phoenicians joined the battle and formed an alliance with one of the native tribes to keep the encroaching Greeks from taking their part of the island.

The Greek settlements on the island managed their business just like those on the southern shores of Italy itself and Greece. But even amongst them, there was tension. The island of Sicily had been settled by two factions: the Ionians and the Dorians. The Ionians maintained a good relationship with the Sicilians and the Phoenicians. However, the Dorians were not nearly as friendly and wanted nothing more than to expand their territory, even if it meant taking land from the Phoenicians and the native Sicilians. Of course, the trade routes and naval capabilities allowed all of these factions to become quite wealthy, which, in turn, allowed the more expansion-minded Dorian Greeks to begin increasing their territories.

By 540 BCE, the Carthaginians had worked their way into control of Sicily. Though there were minor skirmishes, for the most part, the Greeks and Carthaginians seemed to reside in peace during this period of time; that is, until a Spartan prince named Dorieus lost his throne, took his people, and sailed west. He found his way to Sicily, where he asserted his authority and expanded Greek trade and territory. After the passing of Dorieus, the excommunicated Spartan king broke ties and left the Greeks on Sicily on their own. This, of course, meant that those Greeks with power began to seize even more influence.

These power-hungry Greeks turned rapidly into tyrants, with a few of those gaining superior power and ruling the island with an iron fist. Though there was still a division amongst the Greeks along Ionian and Dorian lines, the Dorian Greeks eventually began to overtake the Ionians. Under this rule, the Greek tyrants began a process of removing all the Ionians from their cities through deportation and enslavement, as well as ethnic cleansing. Political moves and alliances were the only cards the Ionians had up their sleeves, but eventually, they needed to reach out for help from their more powerful allies, the Carthaginians, which would begin the First Sicilian War.

When the Persians attacked Greece in 480 BCE, the Carthaginians felt it was the perfect time to make a move on the island, and they did so with the largest Carthaginian military force ever put together. This massive undertaking quickly took care of Theron, one of the Greek tyrants who had seized control of the island. But even with this victory, there was still quite the fight ahead for the Carthaginians before they could call Sicily theirs.

After months of fighting, the Carthaginians were met by Gelo at Himera, which would be the last battle of the conflict. Prince Gelo would ride out of Syracuse, where his father, King Hiero II, sat on the throne, to stop the Carthaginians from moving farther into Sicily. The conflict at Himera would be a bloody battle that would cost many men their lives. The mighty Carthaginian King Hamilcar was mortally wounded during the battle, and the Carthaginians retreated in defeat. Though there was no loss of land on either side, the reparations and the funds secured from the war allowed the Greek presence to flourish.

For seventy years, there was a delicate balance when it came to power on the island. While this peace was maintained, the Carthaginian Empire expanded, encroaching on lands ranging from North Africa to the Iberian Peninsula. In 416 BCE, the peace between the Dorian Greeks and the Ionian Greeks was shattered when the cities of Selinus and Segesta reignited their feud. Like in the previous conflict, the Ionians fell back on relying on their allies for help, but this time, the Carthaginians ignored their pleas. But the Ionians were not left alone, as the Greeks heard their call and responded by sending reinforcements. This, of course, caught the attention of the Carthaginians, and they soon rethought their original stance and joined the battle. However, they wanted to solve the problems with diplomacy. In order to do that, though, they had to bring the Sicilians and Greeks to the table, and the only way to do that was through force.

Diplomacy would be intermixed with battles, and eventually, the Carthaginians would gain control over Sicily and begin the height of their reign. Over the next three centuries, there would be five more Sicilian Wars until Rome finally got involved seriously, causing the first of the Punic Wars to begin. Rome and Carthage would struggle for control over the island, with the Carthaginians and Romans ending up at the negotiating table. Rome would annex Sicily, and because Carthage was the defeated party, it would also have to pay reparations. This, however, was not the last time these two mighty empires would come up against each other in Sicily.

In 215 BCE, a rivalry was sparked by Hannibal's push into Roman territories, one of which was Sicily. For several years, conflicts would rage until the Carthaginian forces were toppled by the Roman forces and the plague. Having taken a hit from all sides, the Carthaginians packed up and went home, leaving the island to the Romans. This rapid departure changed a lot of things on the island, and the biggest of all was the idea of owning land. Romans from the mainland sought to capture some of the prime lands that were now available at bargain prices. For those Sicilians who had supported Carthage and still held tracts of land, they would soon find themselves at the mercy of Roman executioners. In the end, the Sicilians who were left on the island that had been Greek or Roman supporters, together with the Sicilians and Greeks from the mainland, were able to swallow up all the land.

These new landowners had a different mentality when it came to the slave population on the island. With most of them being there as part of the reparations or from other places like Macedonia and other parts of the Mediterranean, the elite had little empathy or sympathy for the slaves. The new landowners' attitudes led to many of them treating their slaves more poorly than normal. Under the influence of power, these men turned to savagery, like starving their slaves and leaving them exposed to the elements by not providing the right clothes for them. An influx of slaves from pirates and the corruption of the Roman governors would lead to even more inhumane behavior.

On top of the squalid conditions that the slaves of Sicily had to put up with, there were elite members of Roman society who found ways to entertain themselves. However, this would cost many slaves their lives. One type of entertainment included setting up manhunts on select estates, where slaves were the prey for these barbarous Roman men. After all, these socialites had an ample supply of slaves steadily coming to their shores, so it was financially beneficial to work their slaves to the bone and simply replace them than it would be to build shelters and make sure they had all the necessities in order to survive.

The poor treatment of these slaves led them to turn to crime in order to make sure they and their families were fed and clothed. Because of the isolation of the island itself, the Romans paid little attention to what was actually going on there. This left the corrupt Roman governors on the island to oversee the situation, and Sicily soon became known as a dangerous destination and a place where one's life was constantly in peril. This atmosphere and the treatment of the slaves would lead to two slaves marshaling their comrades together and rising up against the Sicilian Roman slave owners in 135 BCE. Though these two men would stand up on their own, they would eventually join together and form an alliance that would withstand the Roman onslaught for several years.

Chapter 3 – Eunus and His Prophecy

It was challenging for a slave to elevate their worth in the eyes of their owners. But amongst the slaves of the Sicilian Greek Antigenes was one who was able to do just that. Eunus was born in Syria, and he had a special power that his owner loved to trot out in front of his friends and special dignitaries. Eunus was thought to have the sight, as he was supposedly able to conjure magic and prophesize. (However, some scholars in later years would refute this, saying he was able to command attention due to his charisma.) Many nights, this slave would regale his owner and others with his prophecies and tricks for hours on end. Eunus would do everything from making things disappear and reappear to breathing fire. One of his many tricks was to tell tales and prophecies.

One particular night, he began talking of a future where the Sicilian upper class would feel the pain of the people they abused every day. In his prophecy, Eunus described in detail how the slaves would rise up and topple their rulers and how the upper class would either be killed or enslaved. These slaves would turn to him for leadership, and he would end up on the throne. Most of the slave owners found this quite humorous, and some even gave him tips for this wild tale. Those who opted to award him for his words made a vow that if he ever sat on the throne, they would be safe from both death and enslavement.

Word of Eunus's prophecies soon found their way to the slaves, and in desperation, the slaves reached out for guidance. Like many others, the slaves of Damophilus, a wealthy landowner who dealt out excessively harsh treatment, had had enough. So, a group of them snuck out and found their way to Eunus. Once they found him, they began telling their tales of mistreatment, including being branded and other horrendous torture. They even went on to discuss that the torture was done not only by the head of the household but also by his evil wife.

After listening to their story and being asked what he thought they should do, Eunus responded the only way he could. He informed these beaten-down men that it had come time for his prophecy to become a reality. Eunus told them that the gods were on their side and that they should gather together with other slaves and follow him to Enna, which would be their first victory on the road to overthrowing their cruel masters. When the slaves returned to Eunus, they no longer were just a handful of men. Instead, they now numbered somewhere near four hundred strong.

Amassed before their leader, they pledged their allegiance to him, and they then armed themselves with what they could find. Full of rage, which was specifically aimed at their master, the slaves were spurred on by the encouraging words of Eunus. The slaves were now ready to take the pivotal city of Enna. The city itself was easily taken, as no one suspected this type of attack could have been possible. The slaves mercilessly left few people without a mark. Of those, the fact that they chose to spare the ironsmiths was perhaps the most vital move to the uprising's success. Keeping them alive and their forges intact would allow the slave army to replenish their weapons more easily.

But that wasn't what they had come for, and so, the slaves ripped through the houses of the city, dragging the owners and their families into the street and committing unthinkable atrocities. No one was safe in this rage-filled bloodbath, not even the children. There were accounts of the slaves ripping children from their parent's arms and tossing them viciously to the ground. (This was, of course, written in the history annals of a later time, so no one can be sure if this actually happened; if it did, it was certainly brutal.) The slave army saved the worst atrocities for their owners and the other elites in the city, though. As the slaves ran through the streets, more slaves joined in, creating even more chaos.

As the slaves finished pillaging the city, word reached them that the man who had ignited this flame was holed up outside of the city with his family. This was unacceptable, so the slaves sent a group to collect Damophilus and his family and bring them back into the city to receive their punishment. It took very little effort to overcome Damophilus and his relations. The barbaric master and his wife were tied up. The benevolent daughter of Damophilus was spared by the slaves, as she had always been kind to them. The leader of the mob appointed several men to take the young woman to Catana (modern-day Catania), where she would be placed in the care of relatives. Once she was off on her journey, her parents were driven down the roads and into the city, with insults being hurled at them on their way.

The couple was pulled by their bindings through the streets of Enna and soon found themselves standing in the middle of the theater surrounded by angry eyes and bitter words. Damophilus quickly began to plead with the slaves, using his fine skills of oration. His words began to reach the crowds, calming their fears and turning the tide of opinion. But for those slaves he was cruelest to, they didn't want to wait for the verdict of the masses. They knew they would not get what they wanted, so they took action. Two of his slaves stepped forward, and one of them pierced his chest with a sword while the other swung his ax at his neck. The crowd was startled, but that soon disappeared as a wave of joy swept over them upon realizing that they had succeeded in taking Enna and were now well on their way to freedom.

Seeing that the slaves were all looking at him, Eunus took to the stage and was soon voted in as king. His prophecy had been fulfilled, and it didn't take him long to begin making decrees. Eunus's first action as king was to rename himself, and he chose a powerful name from his Syrian ancestry. He would henceforth be known as King Antiochus. He then called to his people and bade them bring the prisoners forward and ordered them all to be executed except for the wife of Damophilus and the new king's own masters. Damophilus's wife had a fate worse than death. King Antiochus decreed that she would now be the property of the female slaves she had brutally tormented. The female slaves tortured her for a while, and when they tired of it, they sent the woman over a cliff to her death. As for Eunus's owners, he took pride and enjoyment by taking their lives with his own hands.

After all that was taken care of, it was now time for King Antiochus to finish his coronation. He took fine clothing for himself from the homes of the now-deceased upper class of Enna and found a crown as well. Now that he looked the part, he needed a queen, and for this, he turned to the woman who had traveled with him and had been his living companion, making her his consort. King Antiochus then took the men from amongst the mob who had shown some insight and intelligence and created a council to advise him. With all of this now in place, he was ready to continue his rebellion and build a kingdom in which the slaves of Sicily would rule over the Romans, Greeks, and Carthaginians who still resided on the island.

Chapter 4 – The First Servile War

King Antiochus and his slave rebellion was an inspiration to the other slaves on the island, and it didn't take long for a large uprising to begin. In fact, on the southern part of the island, a Roman slave named Cleon would amass a slave army as no one had ever seen. Cleon had found his way to Sicily after being taken captive in his homeland of Cilicia, which can be found in the southeastern region of modern-day Turkey. Because of the poor treatment by his master, Cleon resorted to theft and murder. Cleon had had enough, and he was encouraged by the capture of Enna to reach out to his fellow slaves in the area. It didn't take long before he had gathered somewhere in the area of five thousand men. With his army amassed, Cleon set his sights on taking Agrigentum. The city fell without much effort, just like Enna.

The Romans on the mainland and on the island itself now began to take notice. However, they still didn't have any ideas on how to combat the new problem; they actually thought the two rival slave armies would eventually turn on each other. Unfortunately, this was not to be, as Eunus reached out to Cleon, and the two merged their forces. Cleon proudly stepped into the position of general under the new king. It wasn't long before King Antiochus's army went from a mere 10,000 soldiers to 200,000, at least according to some accounts.

With this massive army, the Roman leadership began to worry and take note. In order to nip this insurrection in the bud, the Roman leadership sent one of their generals to the island as a governor, and he was backed up by eight thousand soldiers.

Lucius Hypsaeus was the first in a long line of praetors sent by the Roman Senate that looked to squash this slave rebellion with ease. But they all were greeted with a mounting army and men who fought for a cause and knew the lands well. Unfortunately, this combination was too deadly, and praetor after praetor failed to get the job done. The unsuccessful campaigns against King Antiochus even spurred slaves in the capital city itself to attempt a revolt; however, this small conclave of slaves failed. This minor disruption gained even more ire from the Roman Senate, though, and in 133 BCE, the mighty praetor Lucius Calpurnius Piso was tasked with the job of ridding Rome of this nuisance.

Piso struggled like the other praetors at first but not in the same way. After being given this duty, he began forming an army that could face King Antiochus's army. But this proved to be challenging, as the Roman citizens had turned against the concept of conscription, and none of the lower classes had any property, which didn't give them an incentive to fight for anything. Eventually, after a lot of hard work, the praetor was able to amass a decent-sized force of soldiers, and they set off for the shores of Sicily. The Roman forces landed in the port city of Messana (modern-day Messina), where they were unsure of how they would be received.

To the praetor's surprise, the people of the city met the Roman legion with open arms. The Roman Senate had hopes that Lucius Calpurnius Piso could take the city without bloodshed, and the senators sent Piso with a decree that gave the city an exemption when it came to levies and taxes on their property. But though the people in the city seemed willing to take this gift and move on, King Antiochus heard of the landing, and he moved his troops toward the city, ready for combat.

Thus, before the city of Messana could be officially taken, Lucius Calpurnius Piso and his legion had to confront the slave army. The two forces met on the battlefield just outside of Messana at Kurkourakis (modern-day Curcuraci). But King Antiochus had underestimated the Roman forces, and the slave army retreated, leaving eight thousand slaves behind as captives of the Roman legion. In order to send a message to King Antiochus and the people of Messana, Piso took those eight thousand slaves and executed them, hanging them in open view of whoever dared to pass by the blood-soaked battlefield. Once these rebels had been taken care of, the praetor moved his legion toward the walled city of Tauromenium (present-day Taormina).

The Roman legion marched to the city of Naxos and then surmounted the hill where Tauromenium sat, planning to lay siege to the mighty citadel. The city, however, was protected by a large contingent from King Antiochus's army, so the Roman legion found this task quite difficult. It seemed that Komanus, the leader of the Sicilian slave army in this outpost and Cleon's brother, was well versed in military tactics, and that, coupled with the well-built defenses of the city, made Tauromenium unbreachable. Fearing that this siege would take too long and cost too much, Piso and his legion retreated and refocused their attention on Morgantina and Enna. (Morgantina was another major city on the island.)

The terrain was treacherous, as the Roman legion led by the confident praetor found itself going west through the remnants of the mighty Mount Etna. But the landscape also worked in their favor, as they found themselves going toward Morgantina through the canyon that housed the Alcantara River. This gave them easy access to water and a definite focal point to watch for potential attacks from King Antiochus's troops. The march to Morgantina took several days, but eventually, the city came into view, and Piso's legions set up for another siege.

Unlike Tauromenium, Morgantina fell pretty quickly. Lucius Piso and his legion were able to break the city, and they took the remaining men of the rebel slave army and crucified them for everyone to see the consequences for standing up against the mighty Roman Republic. With another of King Antiochus's fortresses taken, Piso continued his conquest to reclaim Sicily for Rome. Next up on his agenda was the citadel of Antiochus's power—Enna.

Marching north, Lucius Calpurnius Piso found a strategic location at the bottom of the hill where Enna stood. He set his troops up to once again lay a siege. The Roman general took advantage of the massive flat landscape there and rolled his catapults forward. For days, the Roman forces sent heavy boulders and anything they could get into their catapults to bombard the city.

Peppered throughout the heavy bombardment were many skirmishes, but the Roman forces just couldn't break Antiochus or his troops. Eventually, the slave army was able to deal a death blow to Piso's siege. During a skirmish with one of the Roman leader's cavalry units, the slave army was able to surround the Romans, forcing them to surrender. With this defeat, the Roman forces lost not only men and weapons but also horses. This infuriated the Roman general, and he dealt the leader of the cavalry and the remaining men who returned to the camp a humiliating punishment. The men were relegated to the lowest ranks of the army, and as for the head of the cavalry unit, he was made to stand as Piso's tent guard clothed in rags. He was also not allowed to bathe or wear shoes. Hoping this would inspire fear of failure, Piso made it a point to ridicule the cavalry leader at every turn. But even with his punishment (which did not inspire the fear Piso had hoped) and determination, Enna was impregnable.

Lucius Calpurnius Piso returned to Rome after a year of conquest to stand before the Senate. Though he had some successes, he had to stand in front of his leaders and admit that his campaign had been unsuccessful. Fending off attacks on all sides, the Senate knew that they had to squash the issues on Sicily so they could utilize these forces in other parts of the republic. For instance, they could use those men to shore up their borders in places like Spain, which had been dealing with the Celtiberian uprising. So, the Senate continued sending praetor after praetor in order to remove Antiochus from his throne and regain control of Sicily.

In 133 BCE, the parade of praetors continued with Marcus Perperna. Like his predecessors, Marcus Perperna knew that the answer to toppling Antiochus's regime was to take Enna. So, after his legion landed on Sicily, he immediately began marching toward the citadel. As the Roman praetor's troops neared Enna, they came upon a camp of Antiochus's troops. Knowing that the slave army would have to pass through them and not wanting to have any forces coming to the citadel's aid, Marcus Perperna opted to surround these troops and battle them. The conflict took quite a bit of time, but King Antiochus's troops, starving and riddled with plague, had no choice but to surrender. The Roman leader wanted to send a message to Antiochus, and like the praetors before him, he thought crucifying the remaining enemy soldiers was the way to do that.

Unfortunately, this defeat and subsequent display of power didn't have the desired effect, and Marcus Perperna had to return to Rome with this lackluster victory. After all, this was just one squadron of Antiochus's soldiers, and with their defeat, most of the king's army flocked to his side to protect him and their capital. But the victory was a sign that the Roman forces would defeat Antiochus's entrenched forces, so when Marcus Perperna returned to Rome, he was greeted with a hero's welcome. Knowing that Rome was busy celebrating their meager win, Antiochus ordered Cleon to move on Messana, the main point of access for the Roman troops from the mainland.

Wanting to eliminate the Roman legions' access point, Antiochus's forces moved on Messana, overtaking a large swath of the city, including the fortress and the harbor. The bulk of the city's population was able to find shelter behind the walls, saving themselves from horrible deaths. However, the fortress was quickly fortified, and the harbor was blocked with a chain so that the Roman forces were unable to enter without scuttling their ships. With the taking of Messana, Antiochus's kingdom ranged from the southern coastal region of the island all the way to the eastern coast, leaving very little land still controlled by Roman allies or forces. With these new developments, the Roman Senate had had it with this slave king and his rebels. With this sentiment prevalent in the Senate, they passionately pled with the consuls to play their part and help get rid of the problem.

Of course, the Senate felt they should retake the port city they had just lost, and the consuls that met with the Senate agreed. Two very well-known individuals in Roman politics took up the challenge of overthrowing the slave king. Publius Rupilius and Publius Popilius Laenas were members of a committee that had meted out justice in a recent assassination of a major Roman political figure, and they had built quite the reputation for their fervent love of the republic. Though both were not well known when it came to their military capabilities, as part of the committee, they had garnered many honors, which the two would use to build an army to meet Antiochus's troops on the battlefield. Once the legions had been enlisted, Rupilius and Laenas began their long march south.

Rupilius and Laenas arrived on the Calabrian coast just across the Strait of Messina, but word of their pending arrival had already found its way to the court of Antiochus. In order to combat these Roman legions, Antiochus ordered Cleon to disperse squadrons of their army along the northern coast. Unfortunately, though, Antiochus's troops didn't quite make it far enough north, as the Roman legions of Laenas and Rupilius had already sailed across the strait and found a good base camp in the large inlet known as Paradise Bay. Once Rupilius and Laenas were securely situated in the inlet, they constructed a strategic plan that would utilize the fact they were better equipped than their enemies.

The two consuls separated their fleet into smaller fleets, and these were sent into the harbor of Messana for days on end. This, of course, put pressure on the defensive forces of Antiochus's troops, as it did not allow them any time to recoup after the attacks. Rupilius watched the battles from his ship in Paradise Bay, waiting for the pressure to be too much that it would leave a crack in Messana's defenses. Eventually, his fleet's constant bombardment of the city did just that, and it was time for a land attack. After marshaling his troops, Rupilius pushed his fleet into the harbor, making landfall with his mighty legion.

The days of assault gave the Roman legion the upper hand, and with a bloody push into the city, the forces of Antiochus were overthrown. The streets were strewn with bodies, and there would be many more, as Rupilius was able to take eight thousand slaves as hostages. Rupilius waited for the major part of the battle to be done before he, too, made landfall and continued the savagery. In order to make his victory evident and let the king of the slaves know that he was on his way to him, Rupilius took those eight thousand slaves and nailed them to crosses as he traveled along the coast from Messana to Capo Peloro, leaving them to suffer in the sun. Some died immediately, while others would take days to die. Either way, the message was clear: Rupilius intended to be the one to end this rebellion and return Sicily to Rome.

Rupilius moved toward Tauromenium, taking his legion along the coast. This would be his next big hurdle, as this city was fortified with well-built walls and a legion of Antiochus's men, which was led by Cleon's brother, Komanus. In an effort to have a peaceful surrender, Rupilius offered the city's leaders the chance to surrender, but they were too devoted to their king and their freedom, so they refused. Having no other recourse, Rupilius had his troops dig in for a siege. The Roman forces surrounded the city for days, and with each passing day, the people inside faced dwindling supplies until they could no longer take it. They sent a representative to Rupilius to talk about conditions for a peaceful solution. Rupilius now knew that his plan was working, so he sent the courier back with the answer that nothing short of unconditional surrender would bring his tortuous siege to an end.

This answer was not even an option for the besieged forces within the city. Though there had been rumors of cannibalism and there were sick people everywhere in the city, the former slaves could not see dying any other way than as freemen. Unfortunately for Antiochus's forces in the city, there were those who were perfectly comfortable with the terms. One of the slaves, Sarapion, found his way to the Roman camp and quickly revealed everything that Rupilius needed to break the defenses of Komanus and his troops in the hopes he might be spared.

With this knowledge, Rupilius spurred his legion into action. The strategy was simple: the infantry would charge the walls, using their shields to protect them from the projectiles of their enemies as well as their own forces. Behind these infantrymen, Rupilius instructed his archers and catapults to bombard the city. This tactic put extreme pressure on Antiochus's troops inside the fortress, and eventually, the Roman legions broke through the citadel's defenses. As the legions tore through the streets, Komanus realized all was lost. In an effort to save himself from the fate that awaited him if he was taken hostage, Komanus chose to take his own life.

Rupilius and his troops took the city quickly and once again found themselves in possession of hundreds of captives. These prisoners were tired and hungry, but the end of the siege was not the end of their suffering. Just like he did in Messana, Rupilius wanted to send a message. At Tauromenium, this meant torture and a ghastly end for the prisoners. Once the soldiers and Rupilius were done tormenting their captives, the soldiers marched them to the top of the city's walls and herded them over the edge to their deaths.

Rupilius also found that he had done the impossible—he had captured Antiochus himself. After the city fell, one of the soldiers stumbled upon a pit with a slave hiding inside. The soldier dragged the slave from the pit, and the man was brought in front of Rupilius, who quickly realized who the man was. Knowing that the end of the revolt was near, he sent Antiochus to Morgantina to await punishment. He would not make it to his judgment, though, as the slave king would fall sick and die waiting for his trial.

The rebellion wasn't quite done yet. Rupilius knew he had to take Enna before he could claim utter victory over the slave rebellion. Cleon had barricaded himself in the city's walls, waiting for the impending battle. As Rupilius lined his legion up outside the city's walls, Cleon felt the only way to save himself and his troops was to charge the line. Thinking he could break the lines and flee to safety, he urged his troops out onto the field. Cleon would not find his way to freedom, though; rather, he would perish due to wounds sustained during the conflict.

Without their leader, the rebel troops and the city of Enna fell to Rupilius with ease. The slave army crumbled, and Sicily was once again under Roman control. Once again, Rupilius utilized his captives to deter the slaves left on the island from thinking about ever doing something like this again. Rupilius took over twenty thousand prisoners of war and crucified them as he moved his legions to the coast. He and his legions returned to Rome in victory, and the First Servile War came to an end after three years and thousands of lost lives. But though the war had ended in favor of Rome, the slaves' memories and sentiments of the rebellion in Sicily never wavered. It was just a matter of time before that rebellious spirit was ignited once again.

Chapter 5 – The Cimbrian War: Catalyst for the Second Servile War

It had been twenty-three years since the uprising of the slaves in Sicily had troubled the Roman government. In that time, the Roman Republic had expanded and became a mighty power in the Mediterranean. It seemed that nobody would be able to stop the growth of this powerful empire. But in 113 BCE, the ever-growing Roman Republic would be challenged by a large Germanic horde from the north, which began to migrate into the northern parts of Europe. The migration had actually started two years earlier when the Cimbri began their long southward trek from the Jutland peninsula.

Due to harsh winters and continual flooding of the lands they called home, the Cimbri knew that they had to find a new place to settle, and mainland Europe seemed to be perfect for them. So, the tribe packed up their belongings, and men, women, and children began their long search for a new homeland. As they made the long journey, their numbers began to increase, as hundreds of thousands of people from other tribes (the Ambrones and Teutones, to be specific) joined them in search of a new home. These other tribes were suffering from the same issues that the Cimbri had, and they desperately needed to find a new homeland as well.

In 113 BCE, this caravan had worked its way south and reached Noricum, which was ruled over by the Taurisci. This kingdom, which was located in the northern parts of the Alps, had been ruled by the federation of Celtic tribes for quite a while. But as they looked out and saw the huge masses of Germanic tribes moving toward them, they knew that they were no match for the sheer number of warriors housed within those ranks. Understanding this, the Celtic chief sent word to his ally in the south, which was none other than Rome. Not wanting this Germanic horde to make its way closer to Rome, the Roman Senate agreed to help and soon sent a Roman consul named Gnaeus Carbo to help with the problem.

Carbo, like many other Roman consuls, looked to have his name etched in history and to build his reputation amongst his fellow Roman patricians. With this in mind, he marched his legion into the Celtic tribal lands and set up camp at a strategic point. Knowing that he would have the upper hand, Carbo was shocked when emissaries from the Germanic tribes appeared before him in his tent. The Cimbri had heard through their travels south of the power of the Roman Republic, and they didn't want to end up in a conflict with them. Instead, they approached the Roman consul and bartered for a peace treaty. Carbo only delivered one condition for the treaty, and that was that the Germanic tribes would immediately leave the Celtic territory. The Cimbri complied with this.

Though Carbo had agreed upon a tentative peace treaty, he did not intend to honor this treaty. The Cimbri packed up their people and were escorted by a handful of Roman soldiers from the Celtic lands. However, the Roman soldiers who were given the task to escort the Germanic tribes were also instructed to guide them into an ambush. Unfortunately for Carbo, one of the guides did not want to cause harm to the women and children, and he betrayed the Roman consul.

So, as Carbo's men led the Germanic tribes into what was to be an ambush, he and his men soon found themselves descended upon by thousands of Germanic warriors. In an effort to prove their military might, the Germanic warriors mercilessly killed almost every Roman soldier, but Carbo and a handful of his soldiers were able to escape. Upon returning home, Carbo found that he was to be prosecuted because of his failure. The trial was short and ended with the verdict that he should be exiled. To save face, Carbo took his own life rather than be separated from his beloved Rome.

Rome was now on high alert and prepared itself for more conflicts with this rampaging German horde. The Cimbri and their Germanic brethren continued looking for lands they could settle and make their own. As they moved west into the Gallic lands, they razed and pillaged many different territories. As they did this, many Gallic tribes chose to join them rather than resist. This meant that the threat to Rome was growing larger and looming closer and closer to the center of Roman power. This was unacceptable, and Rome soon began sending legions to combat the Germanic tribes and to bolster the forces of their allies throughout southern Gaul.

The Cimbri horde and its victories over Roman allies and Roman legions empowered smaller tribes in the area. Tribes such as the Helvetti moved against Roman troops stationed in the area of Tolosa. This incursion caused the Roman proconsul (a governor of a province) in charge of the area to mobilize his troops to regain the city. After the victory, Quintus Servilius Caepio, the proconsul, feared that the Cimbri would eventually turn their attention to Rome, so he developed a defensive strategy and waited for the inevitable push toward Roman territories. It didn't take long for the united Germanic tribes to do just that. While the forces moved closer and closer to Rome itself, the Senate opted to move legions north to fortify Caepio's position.

Uncharacteristically, though, the Roman Senate opted to send an untried and inexperienced military leader to do the job: Gnaeus Mallius Maximus. This strategic miscalculation would eventually lead to a devastating loss. The two proconsuls set up camp along both banks of the Rhone River near the Roman city of Arausio, and they both jockeyed for control of the legions. Technically, though, Gnaeus Mallius Maximus had seniority over Quintus Servilius Caepio, but Caepio would not bow down to Mallius's control. Because of this, the battle would be carried out as a two-pronged attack, dividing the forces and leaving them open to disaster.

Mallius sent a picketing group forward, headed by the legate Marcus Aurelius Scaurus, in order to have enough warning of a potential Cimbrian attack. But this small force wasn't enough to withstand the sheer number of Cimbrian warriors who attacked them. Most of the Roman troops of the picketing line were killed. The legate and a few of his soldiers were captured, and they were brought to the king of the Cimbri, Boiorix. Maintaining the Roman bravado, Scaurus stood before the Germanic king and offered to allow the Germanic tribes to retreat from the land or face the consequences of choosing to fight the experienced and powerful Roman forces. Boiorix laughed at this soldier's impotence, and instead of withdrawing his soldiers, he instead had the Roman legate executed.

When word of the picket group's decimation and the execution of one of his respected legates reached Gnaeus Mallius Maximus, he looked to his ally across the Rhone, Quintus Servilius Caepio, for backup. However, Caepio refused to move his troops, as this would mean following the orders of the other proconsul. Word of his stubbornness reached the Senate, and they soon sent word to Caepio that he was to merge his forces with Mallius immediately. Not one to balk at orders from the Senate, Caepio led his legion across the Rhone and set up camp, albeit independently of Mallius's camp.

Caepio was not going to take the chance that Mallius would negotiate with the barbarians or somehow rout them. So, he took the initiative and attacked the Cimbri in their own camp. The Roman leader had not foreseen the might of the Cimbrian defense, so very little planning was done when it came to the actual attack of the camp. The battle was over in the blink of an eye, with Caepio's forces being decimated. The Roman leader was able to escape injury and flee back to Mallius's camp. With Cimbrian warriors following close behind, this left Caepio's camp open to being pillaged and ransacked. Not only was his camp left wide open, but the camp he fled to was also left without defenses as well.

The soldiers waiting in the other camp watched as Caepio's camp was taken, and if the option had been there, they would have fled that very moment. But the camp was backed up against the river, which made it impossible for them to cross easily, especially considering the weight of Roman armor. Unable to escape, the soldiers gathered and attempted to stand their ground. Unfortunately, the might of the Germanic warriors and the ill-advised placement of the camp didn't give the Romans any advantage, and it didn't take long for the Roman legion to be laid to waste. The battle was utterly devastating and a great setback for Rome itself.

Not only was the path deeper into Roman territory open, but at the Battle of Arausio, the Romans had also lost more than eighty thousand soldiers. This, coupled with the other defeats around the republic, was beginning to send the people of Rome into a panic. However, instead of moving deeper into Roman territory, the Cimbrian horde opted to move west and test their luck with the tribes of the Iberian Peninsula. This course correction of the horde gave Rome a chance to reorganize as well as to find someone who was experienced enough to fend off the Cimbrian forces upon their inevitable return.

Chapter 6 – The Romans Need an Army

The answer to Rome's problem came in the form of Gaius Marius, a well-respected Roman general who had returned to Rome from a victory in North Africa. Marius was not only a Senate favorite, but his soldiers were also devoted to him. It seemed as if he was the perfect choice to lead the soldiers who would fend off the Cimbrian forces. With the Germanic tribes raiding and pillaging the Iberian Peninsula, Marius began rebuilding the Roman army. Unfortunately for Marius, it proved more difficult than he had thought to recruit and build a new army. There had already been massive numbers of deaths during the initial conflicts with the Cimbri.

With recruits being hard to find, Marius had to take unheard-of actions in tandem with the Roman Senate changing the rules of the Roman recruitment system. At the beginning of his tenure as the head of the Roman forces, only those who owned land or had money were able to enlist as Roman soldiers. With the changes, Marius and the Senate allowed those who were poor or landless to join the army. The idea of earning a set salary and the promise of land incentivized many men to join the legions. Marius also sent messengers to the outlying territories to build his ranks as fast as possible.

Among the many territories outside of Rome that Marius sent word to was Bithynia (which is now north-central Turkey). King Nicomedes III received the request, but with the Roman tax collectors being so prudent with their jobs, there were no men that he could send since most of the able-bodied men had been forced into slavery due to the harsh taxes. This knowledge was shocking to the Senate, and they immediately moved to change the rules, saying that no freeman in any of Rome's territories or allies should be forced into slavery due to tax collection.

The Bithynian king was not the only ruler to find this demand challenging; in fact, the praetor of Sicily, Licinius Nerva, also had the same problem. With the new decree of the Roman Senate coming down, Nerva sent out a proclamation. This proclamation stated that if there were any slaves on the island who felt themselves wrongfully enslaved due to taxes, they should come forward and present evidence to earn their freedom. Many slaves appeared before him to gain their freedom, and after several days of hearings, more than eight hundred men had proven that they deserved liberation from their masters. In response, many of the prominent Romans on the island banded together to coerce the praetor to reverse his decree and return their slaves to them.

With pressure mounting on all sides and with a sizable amount of money from the Roman elite, Nerva decided to stand against the Roman Senate's decree and retract the freedom that he had given the slaves. A new edict was sent out that stated that all slaves who had received liberation were expected to return to their masters and that any slaves who were still waiting for a ruling were dismissed.

The slaves knew the horrors that were waiting for them upon their return, so they chose to find a central location where they could discuss how they could stand up to this betrayal. The slaves took up residence at the Citadel of the Twins in a grove near Palici lake.

Tired of the poor treatment and emboldened by their recent brush with freedom, the slaves discussed many topics, including the rebellion that was brewing. After this meeting, the slaves disbanded, finding shelter in many of the homes across Sicily. The gathering, though, had lit a fire in many of the slaves, including numerous slaves who were owned by a pair of rich Romans in Haliciae. Led by a slave named Varius, thirty of these slaves united together to take their freedom. Varius knew that freedom was not possible as long as their masters were still breathing, so he urged his small gang to kill their masters. The band of slaves snuck into their masters' home in the dead of night, and while their masters laid in bed, they took their lives.

Once the slaves had freed themselves from their owners, they moved onto farms and homes nearby. As they moved from place to place, the small band grew to a force of more than 120 men. Now with a decent force, Varius and his small army established a base of operations near the town of Engyion. There they prepared themselves for the impending Roman attack by fortifying the already sturdy structure. Over the several days that it took to fortify their location, many more slaves found their way to this bastion of hope. There was no way that Licinius Nerva could allow this to continue, so he took eighty men and moved to meet these slaves.

When Nerva and his men reached the slaves' stronghold, it was very obvious that the rebellion would not be easily squashed using force. So, Nerva used his wits and opted to infiltrate the fortress and conquer it from within. He knew there was a brigand roaming the province that had escaped captivity after being sentenced to death. The man known as Titinius would certainly want his record expunged so that he could live a normal life. With this knowledge, Nerva sent word and was able to procure the criminal's services in infiltrating the slave citadel.

Knowing that the slaves would be suspicious of a single man, Titinius gathered together a small body of slaves and appeared before the gates of the fort. He told the guards that he was looking to join them to take his revenge on the Romans who had imprisoned him. These words were the right ones to gain him admittance into the fortress. Once inside, he was greeted by Varius, who welcomed Titinius with open arms. Upon learning of who he was, Varius quickly suggested that he take charge of the army itself as the general. This played right into Nerva's and Titinius's plan. Now with full control over the fortress and the troops within it, Titinius was in place to make his move.

Titinius suggested that the forces make some sort of move on the enemies sitting outside the fortress. Knowing full well that the soldiers of the slave army would not pose a challenge for the Roman soldiers who awaited them, he maneuvered the troops he had been given control over into the waiting hands of Nerva. The Roman soldiers quickly routed the rebels, killing some during the battle but capturing a large majority of them. Like his predecessors before him, Nerva knew he had to send a message to the remaining slaves in Sicily in order to ensure the rebellion was squashed. To do this, he utilized the classic Roman tactic of crucifying his captives.

The slaves who managed to avoid capture opted to take their own lives instead of being crucified. They hurled themselves from the steep rocky crags above the battlefield. Nerva was bolstered by his victory, as he felt that he had single-handedly stopped the slave rebellion in its tracks. Not wanting to incur any more costs, he dismissed the recently conscripted men in his forces, allowing them to return to their homes and their lives.

In reality, though, this was just the first of many uprisings that would go down in history as the Second Servile War. The remaining soldiers returned to their base, where they were greeted with news of yet another slave uprising, this time on the southeastern coast of the island.

Utilizing the lull in work on the estate of Publius Clonius, his slaves, who were inspired by Varius, concocted a plan to achieve their freedom. Using special signals, the slaves were able to make their way into their master's house. They quietly waited for the right moment to slit the prominent Roman's throat.

In hindsight, Nerva's decision to disband his militia was a mistake. He now had to recall them, which allowed the new slave army to build a force that could rival the Roman forces on the island. Hearing of Clonius's slaves' success, slaves from many estates around the area began to flock to the slaves' encampment along the Alba River near Mount Caprianus.

Nerva knew that he needed to move on the slaves as soon as possible, and that meant taking the shortest route, which was by water. So as soon as he was able to muster the appropriate number of men, he packed his forces onto one of his many ships and began sailing south. As he neared the Alba River, Nerva was struck by a sudden thought—the slave army would be able to see them going past if they came the direct route. So, instead of weighing anchor and attacking from the river, he sailed past the encampment and headed toward the city of Heraclea.

When word of Nerva's vessel passing by reached the slaves, they thought that perhaps the Roman praetor was scared, and this incited many more slaves to join the encampment. Within the week it took the Roman forces to make landfall, the slave army's ranks increased to over two thousand men. When Nerva did reach land, the Roman leaders were quick to inform him of the rapidly increasing forces waiting for him. But Nerva still felt that the training and experience of his troops would make up the difference, and he sent Marcus Titinius with six hundred men from the city of Enna to stamp out this new rebellion.

Marcus Titinius marched his well-equipped and somewhat experienced men toward the slave encampment. He was confident that the battle would be quick and decisive. Unfortunately for the Roman general, the slaves had advantages that he might not have been aware of, such as a strategic position that was easily defendable. Though the slaves were armed with simple weapons like sickles and clubs, they had the passion and drive and were able to withstand the Romans' repetitive charges into their encampment. Eventually, the determination of the slave army won out, and many of the Roman soldiers, feeling that all was lost, dropped their weapons and fled the battlefield. Their weapons now lay on the ground for the slaves to pick up and utilize, not only in this battle but also in the coming ones. The slaves chased after the retreating Romans, and they took their vengeance on as many soldiers as they could.

The resounding defeat of the Roman troops gave courage to many of the remaining slaves to break their shackles as well. Within a week of the slaves' victory, the slave army had amassed around six thousand men and women. With so many now gathered, it became clear that there needed to be some organization and someone at the head of the army. A gathering was called, where these topics were addressed. First and foremost, they needed to have a leader, and after looking within their ranks, the majority felt there was no better man to lead the way than Salvius Tryphon. After all, much like the leader of the previous slave rebellion, Salvius was one of the slaves who began this uprising, and he had played a key part in the victory they had just experienced. On top of that, much like Eunus, the great leader of the slave uprising who had become King Antiochus of Sicily, Salvius had once been a reputed seer. And Salvius was a king himself.

Salvius knew that though the numbers had swollen in their ranks, they would be no match if Rome decided to send more legions to crush the rebellion. He was also fully aware that there were still pockets of the island where slaves had yet to be freed. With this in mind, he began organizing his troops by separating them into three squadrons and appointing a general for each. For the women and children, he assigned them menial tasks, like cooking and tending to wounds. Once Salvius had done this, he made each general march in a specific direction. These generals were free to recruit as many of the slaves as they could. After they had made their circle through their designated area, each of the generals was to return to the same place to join together into one giant army.

After weeks of marching, the generals converged at the meeting point, bringing the men and supplies they were able to procure on their marches. King Salvius now stood at the head of somewhere around twenty thousand soldiers. Along with this, the generals brought plenty of horses, cattle, and sheep in order to supply their newly formed army with everything they needed to defeat the Roman praetor still in charge of the island.

But there was a problem: the men who stood before him were raw and undertrained. So, before Salvius could begin his march on any of the well-fortified cities, he had to train his troops. Now in command of more than two thousand horses, the first order of business was to begin training a calvary. Salvius then began training the infantrymen, arming them with the weapons that had been claimed during the last battle. The first city on Salvius's itinerary was the mighty fortress of Morgantina, as he knew this would be a major blow to the Roman forces governing Sicily.

While Salvius was whipping his troops into shape, Roman praetor Nerva began building his forces as well. He was well aware that Rome's troubles with the rebel slaves were not over by a long shot. By pulling together the remaining soldiers from the last encounter and merging them with forces recruited from the island itself, as well as soldiers sent from the mainland, he was able to amass a legion of ten thousand men. He marched his men night and day in the hopes that he could reach the mighty citadel before the rebels could. However, he was unable to meet his goals, as Salvius and his men had already begun besieging the citadel.

Salvius and his troops solely paid attention to bringing down the citadel, which meant they left their encampment with very little supervision. The Roman general seized the opportunity and surprised the rebel encampment. Making quick work of the camp, he took the supplies that he needed and continued his march to break the siege of

Morgantina. Salvius's troops, who had finally found a secure spot to attack the citadel, received word of the attack on their encampment. In fear for those they had left behind, the slave forces rushed back to charge headlong into the waiting Roman legion.

Even though the Roman general had expected that his enemies would turn on him, he was not prepared for their discipline and strength. He had also not accounted for the fact that some of his men were slaves. Salvius realized this, and he stopped and declared that any slave who wanted to be free should throw down their weapons and join him. Not wanting to live their lives being ruled by others, some of the soldiers within the ranks of the Roman troops began throwing their weapons to the ground. Some broke away and joined the slave king, while others simply fled the battlefield altogether.

Not only did this cause panic within the Roman troops, but it also allowed Salvius to reclaim the supplies and arms that the Romans had procured from the camp they had just raided. As the Roman legions began to flee in fear, Salvius and his troops pursued them. In the end, they were able to capture four thousand Roman soldiers. Once the battle was done, King Salvius and his slave army were able to build their armor and equipment to brand-new levels.

With this distraction taken care of, Salvius's troops returned their attention to the fortress of Morgantina. However, during this time, the Roman general in charge of the citadel was able to fortify his position by offering freedom to the slaves within if they sided with him as opposed to the slave king knocking at their door. The slaves, who were more than likely afraid of the unknown, chose to side with the Roman general. The slaves within the fortress fought with fervor, expecting their leaders to stand behind their words when the battle concluded. Ultimately, the people of Morgantina were able to make King Salvius and his forces pull back from the siege.

With the siege broken, the slaves turned to their masters, waiting for their liberation, but it quickly became evident that they had never intended to live up to their word. The slaves within the citadel then turned and opted to switch sides, taking King Salvius up on his previous offer. By adding these slaves to his ever-expanding forces, Salvius had enough power to take the citadel, sending a strong message to Rome. The slaves of Sicily would not give up easily.

Chapter 7 – The Second Servile War

Salvius's slave rebellion was not the only one that was taking place at this time. On the western coast of the island, another slave was taking inspiration from the recent successes. Athenion was a Cilician (an ancient country that is now located in southeast Turkey) who had elevated himself above the other slaves of his two very rich owners. He was smart, and due to his diligence, he had been given control of two hundred of his Roman masters' herdsmen. Athenion had also begun to build a reputation amongst his men as a leader. Thus, when it came time to stand up and overthrow their masters, the two hundred men were more than willing to stand behind Athenion. His family and the rest of the slaves of the estate, though, were forced to toil away in the slave pits. Athenion knew that after his plan had been executed, he would first unleash the slaves there in hopes their gratitude would lead them to join his cause.

Finally, after hearing of the slave revolt of Salvius and his men, Athenion knew it was time. He sent word to his two hundred men, and without question, they rushed on their masters, killing them. The plan went accordingly, and soon those men and Athenion set upon the slave pits, releasing all the men, women, and children kept there from their shackles. Many of the released slaves decide to stay and seek recruitment in Athenion's army. Within just a few days, that two hundred men grew into thousands, and Athenion began to feel the effects of holding all the power. Athenion gradually went from being the slaves' benevolent liberator and leader to a prophet and messiah. It was all part of his plan, as he knew it would be the only way to control his fellow slaves.

Because of his connection with powers the slaves didn't understand and also because he had freed them, the slaves crowned him king. With this new power added to his already illustrious reputation, Athenion took note of where there were faults in the plans of the previous slave rebellion leaders. He came to the conclusion that their problem was that they took anyone into their army. So, instead of following in their footsteps, King Athenion took special care when evaluating those who came before him. He would take only the bravest, most obedient, and strongest into his ranks. The rejected slaves were sent back to continue cultivating the land and breeding livestock. Athenion knew that famine could be a greater death sentence than the masses of legions being sent to the island.

Now with an army of able-bodied men and a supply train that would keep his men fed well, Athenion knew he needed to make his position more secure. Athenion began to talk of his connections with the gods. He began stargazing more and prophesized that he was foretold to take control over all of Sicily. He would relay to his people that though there would be great battles, his people could rely on him to protect the land and crops since they all would belong to him in the end. These prophecies spread across the region and brought more and more recruits into his army. In time, Athenion oversaw ten thousand men, and he knew he needed a big victory to prove his worth. So, he set his sights on the well-fortified city of Lilybaeum (modern-day Marsala).

The slave army set up camp outside the walls of the mighty city and readied itself for what could potentially be a lengthy siege. For weeks, Athenion and his forces laid siege to the city, and even with their determination and the ruler's prophecies, they gained no headway on cracking the city's defenses. Realizing all was lost, Athenion had to come up with a way to back out of the siege and not ruin his reputation with his people. The slave king looked to the stars and the gods for the right answer. After a long night of stargazing, Athenion stood before his troops and imparted the words he had received from the gods. It seems the gods did not look favorably on the siege and warned that if the siege continued, there would be little hope for a victory. In fact, ultimate disaster would befall the army if they continued. Once these words had been relayed, Athenion's forces were more than ready to break camp and move on to their next conquest.

But while the slave army had been laying siege to the city, its Roman leaders found a way to send word to their allies for reinforcements. The ally that answered the call was King Bocchus I of Mauritania (modern-day Algeria and northern Morocco), but it took his small fleet a while to reach the island. The fleet arrived in the city's harbor under cover of night, and its commander, Gomon, decided to attack immediately. Athenion's troops had already broken the siege and were about to slink away in the night when Gomon and his troops attacked. Surprised, Athenion and his troops retreated as fast as possible. Unfortunately for them, the Mauritanian sailors were fast and well trained. The attacking forces were able to take out a good number of Athenion's troops and return to Lilybaeum victorious.

Although the Mauritanians were victorious, their victory served to cement Athenion's ability to be a conduit of the gods, which helped him continue his reign. Along with that, this defeat also changed Athenion's focus when it came to his plan of attack. He now understood that the fortress-like Lilybaeum would fall all on its own if the slaves within the walls began to believe there was some hope for liberation from their harsh Roman masters. Instead, Athenion began looking at taking smaller cities and country estates. This would give him control over the island's resources, which he could then keep from reaching the citadels. It would be simple to watch them fall one by one without expending his forces or resources.

But it wasn't only the Romans that the newly crowned king had to deal with. Without the strict hand of the Roman praetor overseeing the conditions on the island, the poor freemen were also up in arms. Since they had to feed their families, many of these men resorted to any means necessary to obtain food or money, including robbery and murder. These men didn't care what side someone was on; they just wanted to ensure their ends were met. This resulted in a Sicily filled with pockets of lawlessness. This was challenging, but it in no way deterred either Salvius or Athenion in their efforts. In fact, this served to bolster both armies, as many of these unhappy freemen found their way into the slave army's ranks. These extra troops helped Athenion defeat several Roman forces.

While all of this was going on, Salvius was still making moves to cement his newly formed kingdom. After his siege of Morgantina, he made plans to create a capital. For this, he decided that the best location for his palace would be Triocala (modern-day Caltabellotta). But he knew that he would need assistance. Salvius had heard of Athenion's uprising in the south, so he sent word for the other slave leader to make his way north to him. Though he had heard of Athenion's crowning as king, Salvius still saw himself as the only true king of Sicily, which would, of course, eventually cause problems between the two down the road. But for now, the two alphas were open to working together. So, Athenion sent some of his troops out into the countryside and ordered them to continue recruitment. He then took three thousand men and marched north.

The two leaders met at Triocala. Salvius had chosen this place for its lush vineyard, access to water, and the easy defensive position it would afford his new palace. Once the capital was built and fortified,

King Salvius began to build his government, choosing to use the method of the Romans. These councilmen and lictors (men chosen to act as magistrates and councilors) would often stroll the streets in their purple clothing, jewels, and weapons, making sure the city maintained its respectable reputation. Salvius then immediately ordered his troops and Athenion's to begin construction on his palace. This palace was designed with high walls, a moat, and a lavish estate.

After a while, though, Salvius began to be suspicious of Athenion and his ulterior motives. Feeling that it was only a matter of time before Athenion would challenge him for the throne, Salvius had the southern slave leader arrested and imprisoned for treason.

In 103 BCE, the king received some distressing news: the Roman Senate had found a new candidate in their mission to put an end to the slave rebellion on Sicily. Lucius Licinius Lucullus had just raised his status with his most recent triumph over a slave rebellion in Campania (a region in southwestern Italy). The previous year (104 BCE), Lucullus had been appointed to a praetorship, and in a short amount of time, he found himself on the hunt for a fugitive knight who had instigated a slave revolt. Titus Minucius Vettius was an Eques (a Roman knight) in Capua, a city within the Campania region, who had run into some troubles after falling in love with a slave girl. Unable to fulfill his part of a deal he had entered into with several creditors, Vettius found the answer to his problem in murder. Knowing that he wanted to have clear access to the slave girl, he captured and killed both the creditors, as well as his beloved's master. Vettius then continued his rebellion against the system by releasing and arming the slaves.

To make his claim as the leader of the revolution, the lovestruck knight also proclaimed himself the new king of Campania. This proclamation meant he could make decrees, like freeing the slaves in the region. Many slaves across Campania heard his words and escaped from their masters to join him in Capua. With an army of over six hundred men, Vettius began raiding the region and absorbing any slaves who were freed by the raids. Those that chose not to break their shackles found themselves experiencing the same fate as their Roman masters—death.

News of this uprising finally reached Rome, and the Senate acted quickly to appoint someone to take care of the problem. They chose the new praetor Lucius Licinius Lucullus, and backed by 4,400 men, he began his march to Capua. Vettius had heard that Lucullus was marching on him, so he moved his men to the top of a hill that he felt would give them somewhat of a strategic advantage. Once there, he and his men worked tirelessly to fortify the hill. It wasn't long before the Roman leader and his army approached the location, and the two forces immediately clashed. Lucullus's first attempt was easily repelled simply because of Vettius's smart placement of his troops.

It was clear to Lucullus that he was dealing with an accomplished strategist, so he decided that he would have to use a different tactic. Lucullus sent a message via a spy to Vettius's general, Apollonius, offering him safety and freedom if he were to help the Roman praetor end the rebellion. Apollonius knew that the Roman forces would eventually win out, and he also knew what they would do to the rebels afterward. So, he chose to save his own life and betray Vettius. This division of the slave forces allowed the Roman legion to come out on top.

To save himself, Vettius took his own life after he realized that there was no hope for victory. Lucullus kept his word to Apollonius and returned victorious to Rome. This made Lucullus the perfect candidate to take on the slave rebellion in Sicily. He was outfitted with over sixteen thousand men for this new campaign in Sicily, and he was intent on being victorious.

Accompanied by the respected Roman general Cleptius, Lucullus marched his troops into Sicily, heading toward the capital city of Triocala. Salvius was feeling the noose tighten, so he sent someone to bring Athenion to him from the prison he had been rotting in for some time. The king offered Athenion his freedom and appointed him a general once again. Salvius immediately began picking his brain when it came to the proper tactics they needed to use to ensure victory against the Roman invaders. Salvius felt it would be best to stay in the fortified walls of Triocala, but Athenion said that would be a mistake. Instead, he advised that he and the king's men head out and meet the Roman forces on an open battlefield. Staying in the walls of the capital would open them up to a siege that they may not be able to withstand.

The king agreed, and Athenion rode out with more than forty thousand troops to meet the Roman forces on the open plain of Scirthaea. Athenion set up his camp about twelve miles from Lucullus and began to prepare for battle. Though Athenion had the advantage in numbers, his troops were not as disciplined or trained as their Roman counterparts, so Lucullus felt that he would win in the end.

The two armies spent days executing battles that were very light. Each side quickly felt the fervor of conflict, and growing tired of the light skirmishes, they became locked in all-out combat. During the battle, Athenion felt the rush of battle and mounted his horse, charging headlong into the battle while being backed by several hundred of his cavalrymen. Roman soldier after Roman soldier fell to Athenion's cavalry, and it looked like the slave army was on its way to victory. Then a blow was delivered that would change the course of the battle in favor of the Romans.

As Athenion trampled through the Roman forces, he was suddenly struck down from his horse. A Roman soldier had been able to deal severe wounds to the mighty general's legs. After he had fallen from his horse, he was struck one more time. He just lay there, unable to fight. Seeing this, his soldiers began to panic, and this caught the eye of the Roman soldiers, who were made aware that the slave army's leader had fallen. They then rallied and charged into the fighting with more passion than before. This, of course, exacerbated the panic of the slave army, and it wasn't long before many of them were flying back to the safety of Triocala, watching as the Roman legions began mercilessly killing many of their fellow soldiers.

Athenion was still alive, but he chose to feign death and keep himself hidden until the Roman soldiers had left the battlefield. Under cover of night, Athenion raised himself from the piles of corpses around him and found his way back into the citadel.

Salvius and Athenion convened together to discuss the previous battle, and though they had lost, they felt they had dealt a devastating blow to Lucullus's army. Knowing this, they began to work on the fortifications of Triocala because they knew Lucullus would be on their doorstep soon.

Due to the devastating blow dealt by the slave army, it took Lucullus more than a week to find his way to the slave king's citadel. Athenion stood at the head of his army once again, and he agreed with Salvius that they should prepare for anything, including a long siege. But the Roman praetor and his general wanted to end this rebellion as quickly as possible, so instead of laying siege to the city, they chose to rush headlong into battle. On the wide-open field in front of the city, the Roman legion led the first attack against the rebel army. The battle was bloody, but unlike Scirthaea, the victory went to Athenion's forces. Lucullus's camp was decimated, and they were routed from it as well.

This first devastating loss was to be the first in a long line of attempts by the Roman praetor to take the city. Eventually, Lucullus came to terms with the fact that his soldiers were not going to be able to take the city, and instead, they hunkered down for an extended siege. The siege lasted throughout the year. By then, the Senate finally realized that Lucullus would not be able to defeat the slave rebellion, even though he had succeeded in taking Salvius's life during one of the incessant assaults. The Senate decided it was time for a new leader and ordered Lucullus back to Rome.

Lucullus was devastated by this decision and felt betrayed by his superiors. His disappointment turned into anger upon hearing of the arrival of his replacement. To make his voice heard, the Roman praetor disbanded his horses and had his men destroy any supplies they had left, as well as the siege equipment. Without these, he knew that his replacement, Gaius Servilius, would be less successful than he was.

However, this disastrous decision led to a trial upon his return home to Rome in 102 BCE. Lucullus was charged with abusing his command, and he was found guilty. Lucullus was banished from Rome for the remainder of his life.

With the command of the Roman army now firmly in the hands of Gaius Servilius, he marched his army from Messana to meet Athenion's forces, who had been crowned king after Salvius's death. Servilius moved his troops southwest of Messana, marching headlong toward conflict with Athenion and his troops. Eventually, the two mighty forces clashed, and in their first battle, thanks to the sabotage of Lucullus, the new praetor was at a disadvantage.

After several devastating skirmishes, the slave king knew he had superiority over the Roman legions, and he began to take advantage of his position. Athenion would march throughout the island, laying waste to the country and decimating towns and cities. Eventually, he turned his focus on Messana. He marched on the city and launched a night attack, where he killed many and plundered the city for supplies. The powerful slave king then decided it was time for him to set up his own capital. Athenion marched west, setting up his citadel in Macella, an ancient walled city. He began to fortify the city and build up supplies for his army, knowing that more Roman soldiers would come.

Many things occurred on the Roman side of the conflict during all of this. First and foremost, like Lucullus before him, Servilius found himself unable to stop the slave rebellion and eventually was called back to Rome to meet the same fate as his predecessor. In 101 BCE, another consul was charged with stopping the rebellion and defeating the slave army in Sicily; that man was Manius Aquillius.

Outfitted with several well-trained and experienced cohorts from the frontlines of Gaul that had been sent by Gaius Marius, Aquillius landed on the island, ready to do the impossible. His legion was constructed of veteran soldiers, and thanks to the ravages committed against the people of Sicily, many people joined the Roman ranks. This also included the remaining armies of both of the previous praetors.

As the newly appointed Roman general moved toward the fortified city of Macella, he took the time to train those recruited into his ranks who hadn't had the proper training. By doing this, he had a force that far surpassed Athenion's, as well as any of the previous Roman generals who tried to quell this revolt.

Athenion did not want to repeat the mistakes of any of his predecessors, so he opted to march out to meet the new Roman general on the battlefield. The battle raged on, and eventually, Athenion and Aquillius found themselves in one-on-one combat. The two fought valiantly, but Aquillius was able to maneuver so that he delivered a mortal blow. Athenion collapsed to the ground, and upon seeing this, his troops fell back, with many of them fleeing into the mountains around the battlefield. The Roman general gave chase to the retreating slave army.

With very few men left in the slave army, a new leader stepped up to lead. Satyrus stood in front of the now devastated slave army and spoke to them about their bravery and continuing the fight that Salvius and Athenion had believed so strongly in.

At first, the Roman general decided to use force to exterminate the slave rebellion, but he eventually began utilizing their submission instead. Though he had taken more than twenty thousand prisoners, the rebellion was not over until the leaders were gone and the army was decimated to the point of no return. Though some of the forces made their way into the mountains and continued to be thorns in the sides of the Romans for the next two years, the majority of the slave army was taken prisoner and sent to Rome to fight in the arena against wild beasts. This, of course, included Satyrus, who watched as his fellow freedom fighters were forced to die in the pits against wild beasts. Supposedly, instead of battling the beasts, the slaves killed each other in protest. If this is true, Satyrus certainly would have opted to take his own life instead of being forced to amuse the Romans.

Aquillius returned to Rome victorious, having put an end to the four-year-long war that Rome had fought to regain control of Sicily. Though the war was over and Aquillius was victorious, the same fate would befall him as the previous two praetors. He was accused of mismanaging his forces, but unlike the other praetors, he was acquitted. However, he still had a tragic ending to his story. In 89 BCE, he was engaged in a military campaign against Mithridates VI of Pontus and was captured. According to some ancient scholars, a year later, Mithridates would execute him by pouring molten gold down his throat.

Chapter 8 – Gladiators and Their Lives

During the 1st and 2nd centuries BCE, Rome expanded greatly and had taken part in many wars. Because of this, the growing republic was inundated with hundreds of thousands of slaves from all over the world. These slaves did everything from being household servants to working in the fields, particularly in southern Italy and on the island of Sicily. Slaves led an agonizing life, and due to Roman apathy, they were not even considered people. These men, women, and children were considered property by many estate owners and thus were treated poorly. Of course, even amongst the slaves, there were different tiers, but they all existed in the same category in the eyes of the average Roman citizen.

The mass number of slaves that were brought into the Roman Republic at that time is what brought about the First and Second Servile Wars. These wars were nothing more than civil disturbances to the Roman leadership. They took years and manpower to end, but they were never a serious threat to the republic itself. After all, these disruptions had happened on the island of Sicily, not on the mainland, where the effects and consequences of the conflicts could be felt by the Roman elite. But all that was soon to change when the ramifications of the Romans' treatment of the slaves would finally be felt on the mainland. This time, the slave revolt would be led by warrior slaves, otherwise known as gladiators. To understand the actions of these slaves who would shake the foundations of the Roman Republic, one first needs to understand the life and history of the gladiator.

In the early part of the Roman Republic's growth, armed combat outside of a conflict would not be seen unless soldiers were being trained or there was some event like a funeral. Oftentimes at these funerals, one could watch chariot races, competitions of athletic prowess, and theatrical reenactments of great deeds from the deceased's past. These funerals were major affairs and often were even open to the public. At the early beginning of these grand funerals, the games would be set up close to the tomb of the deceased individual they were looking to commemorate. These would be lavish affairs organized by what was known as a munerator. Eventually, as the popularity of these traditions grew, they became more lavish and required more arrangements. These then included a second individual known as an editor, who acted as the munerator or was an assistant of said individual.

As the years went on, these two titles became synonymous with each other. In addition, these events began to be more widespread, even finding their way into private citizens' homes. Citizens were even able to own their own gladiators as long as they had permission from the emperor. Because of this, the position of editor was raised to a state title.

This tradition of funerals is what gave birth to the larger-scale reenactments that were prominent in the colosseums of the Roman Republic and Roman Empire. And as the legislative powers began to be more and more intertwined with this tradition, it became a note of pride to be able to foot the costs of these games. For the smaller towns, this was done by the quaestors (an official charged with handling the treasury in the Roman Republic). They took a large portion of their own salary and donated it to the small towns or communities they oversaw. When it came to larger-scale events, these were often backed by people in higher positions, including even the emperor himself after the republic fell.

The first gladiator match has been dated to the 3rd century BCE, but gladiator fights didn't hit their peak until the 1st century BCE. With an ever-expanding republic and later empire, more and more soldiers were taken prisoner, making it much easier to keep the ranks of the gladiators consistently replenished.

In fact, many of the gladiator categories took on the name of these enemy prisoners. Among these include the Thracian, the Gallus (named after the Gauls), and the Samnite. Each of these categories had a specific look and specialty that would make them stand out in the gladiator matches. The Samnite was a gladiator that came out into the arena in full armor; this category eventually became known as the secutor. This form of gladiator wasn't the only one that got a new name as time went by. For instance, the Gallus was rechristened the murmillo.

The games would progress in many different ways; for example, some of the matches had pairings. At the beginning of these labor-intensive spectacles, one would watch gladiators fighting gladiators who had the same fighting style. But as time went on, people wanted to see more novel fights. Thus, it would not be odd to find a retiarius fighting the fully armored secutor. A retiarius would be lightly armored and use a net to ensnare his opponents and a trident to stab them.

Because of the ever-growing popularity of the gladiators themselves, as well as the games, the trade market for slaves boomed. Many of these slaves would find their way not only to the amphitheaters but also to the mines. However, the best of these warrior slaves were naturally sent to Rome, where they spent their life (however short it may be) training as gladiators and working to gain their honor back.

Of course, enslaving enemy warriors was not the only way the Romans maintained the ranks of the gladiator schools. There were also those known as the damnati, people who had committed crimes and been sentenced to fight in the games. Along with these individuals, there were also people who volunteered to be part of the games (known as the auctorati). Sometimes, becoming an auctorati was the best option available for those of the lower classes or individuals who were noncitizens. By signing up for a gladiator school, these individuals not only learned a trade but were also given room and board. Along with this, there was the option of gaining fame and fortune, which would allow them to pull themselves out of poverty.

The iconic image of a gladiator is of a well-muscled man adorned with armor fighting in an arena surrounded by cheering crowds. But men were not the only ones to fight in the arena. In fact, many women found fame in the gladiatorial battles. They didn't become more popular until the Roman Empire, but their popularity lasted all the way to 200 CE. Emperor Septimius Severus decided that it was inappropriate for women to fight and banned the use of female gladiators (also known as gladiatrix). There were also even emperors, such as Commodus, who took the opportunity to stand in the arena and show their prowess on the battlefield.

As the gladiators' popularity grew during the Roman Empire, gladiatorial fights became a way for the emperor to show his people that he cared about them. At these events, he not only would generously host these fights to entertain his people, but he would also show himself, giving him better visibility. The spectacles became so ingrained in the Roman people's lives that in 70 CE, it became evident to Emperor Vespasian that there needed to be a larger arena so more of his citizens could take in the games.

This thought became the ember that would build one of the greatest amphitheaters ever seen in the world: the Colosseum of Rome. The Colosseum took ten years to build and was christened by a one-hundred-day celebration that was offered to the Roman people by Emperor Titus, who completed construction on the amphitheater.

Even before the mighty Colosseum was built, there were many gladiators spread throughout the country who were learning their skills at schools. Soon, many gladiator schools (known then as ludi) across the republic were opened. In these schools, criminals and prisoners that had been taken during conquests were taught the skills needed for competition in the amphitheaters across the country.

Before their training commenced, there were a few steps that had to be taken care of to ensure that the gladiators knew their duty and their place. These men would swear an oath, dedicating their lives to their training and their masters. For those who had been condemned, they would be marked with either a tattoo or branding so that wherever they went, they knew their crimes and their punishment. At these schools, men were trained on the sandy floors of arenas to not only handle one-on-one combat but also fights against wild animals. Each of the gladiators would be trained in a specific category depending on their method of fighting. For those who were captured in battle, they were often allowed to utilize the weapons they were most familiar with, but for those who had no skills, the master would have to evaluate them. Once they had been evaluated, they were placed in a category and trained to fight in that style.

The novice gladiators would train under experienced gladiators within the school, and through hard work and dedication, they would make their way up the ladder in an attempt to reach the highest rank: primus palus. Regardless of their ultimate rank, each of these gladiators would endure harsh training, gradually becoming mighty specimens that would entertain the masses. During training sessions, they never used lethal weapons. It almost seems like they were rehearsing for a play, a play in which men might die. It was best to have no emotion if such a thing were to happen, as it would help to prove their strength.

To some, this may seem like a glorious way to live and die, but the daily life of these gladiators was very different than the spectacle of the arena. These beloved celebrities were still nothing more than slaves and tended to be locked away at night in cells that were little better than a common jail. These cells were crafted in barrack-like buildings around a training area. Each barrack was dedicated to a certain division of gladiators. The masters of the schools were very careful to ensure that gladiators who may become opponents were kept separate from each other in order to reduce the risk of any potential issues arising both in and out of the arena.

These men were woken at the first sign of light every morning, and their day began with a hearty meal. Even though they were slaves, gladiators were allowed better nourishment and lived in more hygienic conditions than your typical slave or even average Roman citizen. After all, their performance was what made their masters money, so an undernourished and sickly gladiator would be counterproductive. Gladiators also had to endure trials and tribulations that made their life challenging and maddening. These mighty warriors were unable to speak except during mealtimes, and when they were not training, they were often kept shackled. When it came to hygiene, their owners wanted to eliminate the chance of disease, so gladiators were allowed to take hot and cold baths. They were also fed three times a day to ensure their health remained at optimal levels. These meals typically were heavier in vegetables and grains than meat, though they were fed fish and meat.

As mentioned above, the health of the gladiators was very important to their masters, as they were a big investment. This meant that they needed to keep their property healthy, and that included things like regular massages and access to physicians of the highest standard.

Once a gladiator had been fully trained, they, along with their families, were then sold to the highest bidder and continued their existence, fighting for whatever Roman noble had paid for them.

No matter what type of gladiator one was or how one found their way into the school, the danger and excitement that these spectacles created gave the Roman people something to think about other than their difficult everyday lives. That is why during the 1st century BCE, most people, no matter their status, spent their downtime attending gladiatorial games, which quickly became the most popular form of entertainment.

But the spectacle was so much more than just the matches in the arena. There was order and systems put in place to ensure that the spectators got what they came for.

Like the spectator sports of today, the preparations for these games started with advertising. For the layperson, this meant sending out word of who was putting on the event, as well as where, when, and the number of gladiators that were going to be present. These also often contained things like notices of executions and the music and other events that would be going on during the game. Music was a big part of the gladiatorial games; it would even be played during the interludes to keep spectators amused and calm.

Oftentimes outside of the venue, there would be people selling food, drinks, and other novelties. For those spectators who were inclined to bet on the gladiatorial outcomes, they were issued different programs that talked about the pairings, as well as the records of each gladiator.

The night before the events, the gladiators themselves were thrown a great feast and given time to take care of their personal affairs. It seemed that this was intended to be the last meal in case they didn't make it out of the gladiatorial games the next day.

Like the systems in place before the game, the actual gladiatorial events had more pomp and circumstance than one might think. Depending on the era, this might include a procession of important magistrates and men in high positions. After this came trumpeters and idols of the gods, as well as a scribe and other individuals meant to honor the events. At the back of that procession marched the gladiators that were set to fight that day.

Typically, the gladiatorial events would begin with matches that involved wild beasts captured in far-off lands. This would be followed by executions and occasionally warm-up matches for the gladiators. Then the gladiators would come out to entertain the crowd. The spectators were more enthralled when the gladiators were evenly matched. Depending on the type of gladiator competing, these matches often took anywhere from ten to twenty minutes at a time. Those gladiators who fell short of courage and hesitated to enter the arena would find themselves in a world of pain, as the punishment for this was being whipped or prodded with hot irons.

These warrior slaves had rules they had to follow, and because of this, referees were present to ensure that they were doing just that. A match was only won when one gladiator submitted or was killed. For those who wanted to submit, they simply would raise a finger in the air to the referee. This request was weighed for its entertainment value. For the most part, though, the wish to submit was granted. However, this might bring dishonor upon the gladiator, as the more respectable end would be death.

If a gladiator was deemed to have died a good death, they were ceremonially removed from the arena on a couch and taken to the morgue. These respected gladiators would then have the armor removed to ensure they were actually dead, and they may have had their throats cut as well. The bodies of those deemed to have died a disrespectful death were removed and often thrown into a river or a dump, where they would be left unburied for wild animals to desecrate.

The life of a gladiator was not a glamorous one, nor was it one that lent itself to a long life. Gladiators usually only lived to see their mid-twenties, and it is thought that as many as 400,000 lost their lives in the arena. So, it is easy to see why men who had fallen into this situation would find it unbearable and eventually rise up to take their lives back.

Chapter 9 – The Gladiators Who Would Shake Rome

Much like other slaves, many men within these schools dreamed of freedom and being able to live their life on their own terms. This passion and desire led the gladiators of the Capua school to rise up and take their freedom back. In 73 BCE, while the mighty Colosseum was still being built, one of the gladiator schools in Capua (which was over one hundred miles southeast of Rome) encountered trouble. This school was run by Lentulus Batiatus (also known as Gnaeus Cornelius Lentulus Vatia). Lentulus's school took in predominantly Gallic and Thracian slaves to train as gladiators. However, he was a cruel master. He kept his gladiators confined almost at all times and gave them the bare necessities. It took weeks and cunning for the two hundred gladiators to plan an escape that would ensure their freedom. However, somehow, their master found out about this plan and began to act accordingly.

Upon realizing that their plan had been discovered, more than seventy of those gladiators, including a Thracian man named Spartacus who was to become the icon of this revolt, took it upon themselves to act quickly. Grabbing knives and spits from the kitchen, the gladiators rushed through the school and found their way out.

Once free of the walls of the school, the gladiators knew they had to find a way to slow down the mob that would inevitably come after them. This meant they needed to arm themselves better, so they found a handful of wagons that just so happened to be carrying weapons to gladiators in another city.

Taking advantage of their good luck, these men seized the wagons and quickly got out of the city, moving to a more strategic location where they could defend themselves. The escaped men fought off the small force that was sent after them and then found their way into the countryside. As the well-trained slaves worked their way into the mountains surrounding the area, they found it necessary to plunder estates so that they could clothe and feed themselves. Along the way, their small band grew, as they took in slaves from these estates and armed them as well. The escaped slaves eventually made their way into the mountains and set up camp on the slopes of Mount Vesuvius.

Now free and in a position that they felt was easily defendable, the next step was to establish some kind of leadership. For this, the escaped slaves turned to the men who had been the masterminds behind the escape plan: Crixus, Oenomaus, and, of course, the Thracian instigator Spartacus. These men would not only lead the slaves over the next two years but would also grow this small band of slaves into a mighty army of more than 120,000 men. These forces would defeat Roman leader after Roman leader and leave history with unforgettable scenes of horror. The impact of this slave uprising would be felt for centuries, and it would be the catalyst that helped transform the Roman Republic into the mighty Roman Empire.

The Thracian Spartacus was the first leader the slaves appointed. There are many interpretations of who this gladiator was and from where he came. Most scholars believe he originated from one of the nomadic Thracian tribes (most likely the Maedi tribe). The Thracian lands had been ruled over by many empires, and they spanned a good portion of what is now southeastern Europe (countries like Bulgaria, Greece, and even a portion of northwest Turkey all resided within the borders of Thrace). The warriors of this proud race were prized in war and rode alongside many of the great conquerors of the time like Alexander the Great (356 BCE–323 BCE). After the Third Macedonian War, which ended in 168 BCE, the region was swallowed up by the expanding Roman Republic. But it wasn't until 46 CE that it actually became a Roman province.

It may have been during one of the many uprisings in the Thracian region that Spartacus found himself in the Roman military. (Though how he arrived there depends on the historian; some state that he signed up voluntarily, while others think he became a mercenary who eventually found his way into the legions.) Most agree that at some point, he wound up becoming a prisoner, and because of his prowess and physique, he eventually was sold to a man who would later train him to be a gladiator.

The other two leaders appointed by the slave army were both from the Roman territory of Gaul. Crixus, who eventually became Spartacus's right-hand man, and Oenomaus had both been taken during one of the many skirmishes between the native tribes of the area and Rome as it began to expand. Gaul was part of the western European front, and though many different tribes called it home, the region was primarily settled by the Celtic and the Aquitani tribes. (Gaul would have been located in modern-day France, Belgium, Switzerland, Luxembourg, and even parts of northern Italy, the Netherlands, and Germany.) By the middle of the 2nd century BCE, Rome had conquered a good portion of the region; however, it would not be completely conquered until Julius Caesar arrived on the scene in the 1st century BCE.

Crixus was Gallic, and he most likely fell into the hands of the Roman legions during one of the many battles that took place in Gaul. Crixus had a warrior's physique and experience in warfare, so he found himself being sold into servitude as a gladiator.

The last of the triumvirate to be elected as the leader of the rebellion was Oenomaus. Truthfully, little is known about this gladiator except for the fact that he hailed from Gaul. Like the other two men, most historians believe that this warrior was taken at a young age and sold into slavery, where he eventually found his way into the gladiator school in Capua.

With the task of naming their leaders completed, Spartacus and his forces settled into their camp on Mount Vesuvius. Their camp had a narrow entryway, and there was only one way in. The fortified area was also surrounded by steep crevices on all three sides. From here, the slaves would continue plundering the cities and towns nearby.

Eventually, word of the rebellion found its way to the capital, and soon one of the local praetors, Gaius Claudius Glaber, along with three thousand Roman militiamen, marched on the rebel encampment. Glaber came from a plebeian family and had worked his way up, being elected a praetor in 73 BCE. This uprising would be his first test of prowess, and he intended on making the most of it. Though his militia may have been large, they had yet to see battle and had little to no training. This is because the militia was typically only used for riots or to break up fights.

Glaber knew that his troops were ill-equipped to fight any type of ground battle, so he set up camp at the only entrance up the mountain and laid siege to Spartacus and his men. The Roman praetor and his men would wait patiently to hopefully force the slaves to surrender via starvation. Spartacus's forces were just as green as the troops led by Glaber, but they had something the Roman forces didn't—resourcefulness. Although the rebellious slaves were surrounded on all sides by sheer cliff faces, these cliff faces were covered with long vines that could easily be cut and fashioned into ropes and ladders. Spartacus ordered the men to begin cutting them down and twisting them into ladders that could hold their weight. These ladders would have to be long enough to be able to reach the bottom easily.

The Roman forces were, of course, unaware of the ingenuity of these slaves, so they were unprepared for the attack. Spartacus and his men waited until the sun had gone down. Utilizing their cleverly crafted ladders, they shimmied down and moved around the edge of Vesuvius until they had found themselves behind the Roman camp. As the rebel slaves worked their way around to the camp, they found themselves joined by herdsmen and shepherds from the surrounding area. They quickly dispatched what few militiamen were left to guard the parameters of the camp and rushed on the remaining portion of the camp, easily taking care of the militiamen, who were caught off-guard. Glaber and his militia had been defeated by Spartacus and his men, but the Third Servile War was far from over.

Chapter 10 – The Third Servile War

Rome was irritated, but the government was unwilling to look at this uprising as another war, although that attitude would soon change. The Senate was devastated at the loss of Glaber and quickly sent another praetor to bring the rebel gladiators down. The senators decided that Publius Varinius was the man for the job. Varinius chose to send two armies under separate lieutenants to meet the rebels. These forces were led by lieutenants Lucius Furius and Lucius Cossinius, and each rode forward at the head of two thousand men (it is not known whether these men were Roman legions or militiamen). Unfortunately, they would find that Spartacus's forces had greatly increased. It is believed the gladiator general was now in command of more than four thousand people, and he was ready and waiting for Varinius and his generals.

Not only did Spartacus have more men than the praetor expected, but the slave army also had the tactical advantage, as they were very familiar with the terrain. Varinius and his Roman troops trudged through the damp fall weather toward Vesuvius, and along the way, they found another enemy amongst their ranks. As they marched, many of Varinius's soldiers began falling ill, and that, combined with loyalty issues amongst his ranks, would play a big part in his final defeat. On top of this, like many of the Roman praetors who were sent to quell the slave uprisings, Varinius looked at his enemies as weak and unworthy of meeting him on the battlefield. Spartacus was aware of the disdain the Romans held for him and his fellow slaves, and he intended to decimate any Roman forces that he came up against.

The Roman praetor first sent out Furius with his squadron of two thousand men to meet Spartacus near the base of Vesuvius. Furius's men were easily decimated by the slave forces. Spartacus had men constantly surveilling the areas near the mountain, so he was also able to locate another party of Roman troops that intended to attack him. Caught off-guard, Cossinius and his men fought bravely, but they were able to overcome their attackers. Those left alive, including Cossinius himself, fled. The Romans were unable to grab all of their equipment and supplies because of the sudden attack, so Spartacus and his men seized everything that had been left behind before giving chase.

It didn't take Spartacus and his soldiers long to catch up with the Romans, and eventually, the majority of the Roman soldiers were overpowered and killed by the slave army, including Cossinius. With the praetor's lieutenants easily dispatched, Spartacus turned his army to the south and continued to add to his ranks as he traveled.

Varinius was unwilling to take this defeat, so he marched his troops southward as well, running straight into Spartacus's forces in Lucania. Spartacus and his men were already in battle formation, and upon seeing this, many of the praetor's men refused to attack. Some of them even fled. Undeterred by the dissension in his ranks, Varinius pushed on with his remaining men. To the Roman praetor's surprise, the men that he met on the battlefield were better trained and more focused than he had anticipated.

The troops led by Spartacus ripped through the Roman forces with inhuman strength and speed. Varinius watched as his men fell, slaughtered by those he thought were beneath him. Upon seeing this, he turned to retreat. But as the Roman praetor turned, he came face to face with the gladiator general and was soon felled from his horse. Although Varinius was not mortally wounded, he lost his prized horse and had to flee for his life.

Spartacus wanted to take this humiliation one step further in order to avenge the loss of one of his fellow leaders, Oenomaus. He took the captured legionnaires and delivered punishments that seemed fitting to him. Many of these men were put in an arena and made to fight to the death, a fate that would have awaited him and his fellow gladiators. For those who didn't receive this punishment, Spartacus chose Rome's favorite form of punishment: crucifixion. This ultimate humiliation made its way to the ears of the Roman Senate, and they finally realized they had to take the threat more seriously.

Spartacus and his men continued to raid and attack Campania, destroying whatever Roman forces were left there by Varinius. This meant decimating the Roman forces left under the control of Gaius Thoranius, Varinius's quaestor. As Spartacus continued his raiding of the southern regions of Italy, his forces continued to grow. Though there were many skirmishes during the winter months of 73 BCE and the early part of 72 BCE, Spartacus mostly focused on training the men and finding ways to equip and supply the ever-growing ranks of their army.

By this point, Spartacus's slave army had accrued several wins over the mighty Roman military, but those battles had been against mostly untrained and inexperienced soldiers. The gladiator general knew that his forces weren't ready to stand up against the more seasoned soldiers who were bound to come their way. For this reason, he put forth the idea of marching to the Alps, which were well out of the range of Rome's more experienced forces. However, he wasn't the only leader amongst the rebellious slaves, and Crixus stepped forward with his own plan. The Gallic warrior was bolstered by the recent victories against the Roman militia, and he believed that they should use this momentum and head straight for the serpent's head: Rome.

The two contradicting strategies left the bulk of the slave army divided. Unable to come to some sort of compromise, the two leaders broke ties and followed their own paths. Crixus took thirty thousand men (this included a small group of Germanic and Gallic gladiators) and broke away, looking to not only march on Rome but also to continue raiding the villages and towns of southern Italy.

With this division of the slave forces, Rome could no longer scoff at the slave uprising as a simple outbreak of disobedience. The spring of 72 BCE would see two more Roman generals attempt to disband the slave army. These Roman generals were given command of four legions in order to complete this mission. The first of these commanders to see battle was Lucius Gellius.

Gellius had begun achieving his political ambitions at a young age; he spent his youth climbing up the ladder until he was eventually elected as a quaestor in 102 BCE. Still hungry for more, the young man continued to look for more responsibility, and this led him to the position of aedile (these individuals were appointed to maintain public buildings and regulations during public festivals) in 96 BCE. He would continue his climb until he found himself a consulate in 72 BCE, where he aligned himself with Gnaeus Pompeius Magnus (better known as Pompey or Pompey the Great). Gellius was eventually given control of a sizable force by the Senate, which expected him to easily take care of the slave revolt.

Spartacus may have been more challenging for this general to find, but Crixus and his forces were making their presence well known, as they were raiding and rampaging through the small cities and towns of southern Italy. Thus, Lucius Gellius opted to start with this faction of the slave rebellion. He sent two of his legions to the Apulia region (an area in the southeastern corner of Italy) to deal with the rebel gladiator. Leading these forces was the praetor Quintus Arrius, who was to become the next governor of Sicily. However, before doing so, he had to take care of Crixus and Spartacus. Gellius believed that the praetor could march fast enough to lock the gladiator and his army in place with the ocean to their back, so he was confident that his forces would be able to rout this portion of the slave army.

The Roman forces were indeed able to make good time and keep their presence relatively unknown. Near Mount Garganus, the Romans mounted a surprise attack on Crixus and his forces. Crixus and his men found themselves boxed in, and they had to fight ferociously to escape. Unfortunately, they were no match for the Roman legions that they met on the battlefield, and more than half of Crixus's men were cut down. Tragically, amongst the death toll was Crixus himself. Once word of his friend's demise reached Spartacus, he was enraged. While the massacre of his fellow gladiator and his men had been going on, Spartacus had set up camp in the Apennines (the mountain range that runs through the center portion of southern Italy, from the tip of the boot to the top of the leg).

Spartacus spent the winter months training and building up their supplies. He spent a lot of time sending his men out on foraging missions in the surrounding area. These missions included plundering estates and towns and looking for horses to build a better calvary. Spartacus knew that having a well-trained and extensive cavalry could make a major impact in his battles with the Roman forces. It would also make his army's trek to and through the Alps much easier. As Spartacus's men ransacked towns like Consentia (modern-day Cosenza), their ranks grew as well, as more and more slaves were freed from their oppressors. By the time the winter had ended, Spartacus had amassed around seventy thousand people in his army. These slaves, if capable, were given weapons and trained in combat.

As winter began to thaw into spring, Spartacus and his army began moving north, with both Gnaeus Cornelius Lentulus Clodianus and Lucius Gellius hot on his trail. Clodianus had set up north of the gladiator's camp and was hoping to meet Spartacus on his way into the Cisalpine region. The consul, much like his partner in this mission, Lucius Gellius, found himself aligned with Pompey. Having served under him in Hispania, Clodianus had gained his favor and eventually used these connections to be elected as a praetor in 75 BCE. Keeping his eye on the prize, Clodianus was eventually put into the position of consul in 72 BCE. He would then work to bring about Pompey's interests in the Hispania region of the republic until he was called upon to join forces with Gellius to combat Spartacus and his rebellion.

Lucius Gellius, who had dealt with Crixus in the south, looked to take Spartacus from behind while Clodianus blocked Spartacus from moving any farther north. The two consuls hoped to trap Spartacus in the middle, which would allow them to overrun him more easily. As Gellius moved from the south, he came upon a small group of Spartacus's horses that had found themselves cut off from the rest. Some of the slave warriors had drifted away from the main body of the army and were quickly surrounded and decimated by Gellius and his Roman legions as they moved north to meet Spartacus's main forces.

Clodianus chose to utilize the same course of action as Gellius had in the south with Crixus and set about attempting to surround Spartacus and his men. But Spartacus's numbers were far superior, and he turned his forces on Clodianus's legions, attacking them without delay. This maneuver was unexpected and threw the general off-balance, leaving Spartacus with the upper hand. Attacking ferociously and without mercy, Spartacus eradicated a large majority of the Roman soldiers, and this threw Clodianus into a panic, causing the remainder of the troops to retreat.

By the time the battle had ended, Gellius's troops had closed in on Spartacus's rear flank. By turning his forces around and utilizing the same strategies as he had with Clodianus, Spartacus was able to defeat Gellius as well. Without a new plan of attack, the Roman consul fled. Spartacus and his forces were able to capture more than three hundred Roman prisoners. Just as before, he sentenced some of them to fight in gladiatorial combat until the death. He crucified the others, all in the name of honoring his fallen brethren Crixus.

In the meantime, the two consuls would regroup and begin planning their next offensive against the expanding slave army. To do this, the two consuls fled to Rome, where they recruited more men for their armies. Realizing that they were unable to defeat the gladiator general on their own, the two consuls then merged their forces and moved to meet Spartacus on a new battlefield.

Spartacus was undeterred from his prior mission and marched his troops toward the Alps. As he traveled, more and more slaves and gladiators, as well as shepherds and other peasants, joined his ranks. It is believed that there were about 120,000 people following Spartacus as he marched into Cisalpine Gaul (northern Italy).

But when they reached the city of Mutina, they were greeted by the governor of the region, Gaius Cassius Longinus, and ten thousand men. Cassius had just been placed in power as the proconsul of the region after spending several years working his way up the ranks of the Roman elite. The governor had little to no experience on the battlefield, so he kept close to the Roman praetor Gnaeus Manlius. The two rode out to meet the slave horde, but they were no match for Spartacus and his men. Spartacus and his mighty slave army overtook Cassius and his men, killing most of them. Cassius and a handful of men were somehow able to escape the Battle of Mutina with their lives.

The path to the Alps was now completely free of obstacles, but after having tasted so much success, many of Spartacus's men fell back, believing, as Crixus had, that the true route to utter victory involved taking their fight straight to Rome. And it seems that Spartacus may have agreed with them. While it is not known for sure why Spartacus didn't cross the Alps, it is likely that he believed he could take on Rome or that he wanted to prevent dissension in the ranks or the division of his forces. Regardless, Spartacus abandoned his plan and turned south to march on Rome. In order to make this march easier on him and his men, Spartacus ordered his men to kill any remaining prisoners and any excess pack animals to lighten the army's load.

It was one thing for this band of slaves and gladiators to have beaten militiamen and untrained generals, but the slaves inflicting defeats against such well-thought-of Roman generals as Lucius Gellius and Gnaeus Cornelius Lentulus Clodianus was a crushing blow to the Roman Republic. The Senate now knew it had to do something drastic. However, Rome was experiencing a shortage of generals and men, as many of them were stationed in outlying regions of the republic, like Spain and Asia Minor. With no sitting Roman military commander close at hand, the Senate had to look within the ranks of the elites for someone they felt had enough prowess to defeat Spartacus. For this, they turned to Marcus Licinius Crassus, who was a wealthy landowner and had learned much under the tutelage of the Roman general Sulla (Lucius Cornelius Sulla Felix) years prior. That, coupled with Crassus's lineage, made him the perfect choice.

Marcus Licinius Crassus had been born with a bright future, as he was a part of one of the most respected families in Rome. He inherited the family fortune after tragedy struck his older brother and father; he also married his brother's wife, a circumstance that was unique even back then.

However, Crassus's family had supported Sulla during his civil war. Although Sulla was victorious, he left Rome, which was retaken by the opposition. The Roman Senate then placed proscriptions on those who had supported Sulla. In order to get out of these punishments, Crassus fled to Hispania. He called this region home for several years before moving on to Greece, where he eventually found a position in Sulla's army during his second civil war. Crassus, along with other men, such as Pompey, found fame while learning the art of war under the mighty Roman general.

After returning home to Rome, he found that all of his family's lands and wealth had been auctioned off. Crassus quickly set about working on rebuilding his family's reputation and wealth. He also had many other interests, such as developing the first Roman fire brigade and working on building a political career. His dedication and determination paid off with the Senate's appointment of him as the head of the Roman legions. And it wasn't long before intel reached Crassus's desk that informed him that Spartacus was nearing Picenum. (The gladiator had been utilizing the central Adriatic coast to work his way toward Rome.)

Crassus rolled out and set up camp at the borders of the region and waited for Spartacus and his army to reach them. Cassius ordered one of his lieutenants, Marcus Mummius, to take two legions and position himself a distance behind the slave army and hold that position until otherwise instructed. Mummius was also born into a wealthy family, and he was looking to gain favor politically as well as militarily.

Due to this sentiment, he disregarded the orders of his superior, as he felt he had an opening that could lead to a victorious defeat of Spartacus and his men. Charging forward, the lieutenant and his men were easily pushed back, and he lost many of his men during the battle. Crassus didn't sit idly by while Mummius was being attacked; he urged some of his men on to assist the lieutenant in his ill-advised attack. In order to not lose all of them, Mummius ordered his men to throw down their weapons and retreat. This gave Spartacus another opportunity to build his supplies, and it ended up being a disastrous and humiliating defeat for Mummius.

Mummius returned to the ranks of Crassus's legion, where he was received with disappointment and anger. Crassus quickly rearmed the remaining soldiers of the defeated legion and instructed them to give a solemn oath that they would never drop their weapons again. But this slap on the wrist could not be the only consequence for the legion. To prove a point, Crassus gathered together five hundred of the men (most of whom were identified as those who had fled first) and had them divide into fifty ten-man groups. The groups were then instructed to draw lots, and the one that came up short would be executed on the spot. All of the legions were forced to watch this, as it was a clear message of what Crassus intended to do to any legionnaire who decided to be disobedient or a coward.

Now that his men understood what discipline was, Crassus set about retraining and rearming those troops he had left. He wanted to make sure that every one of his legionnaires was adept with the short sword, and he also began training them with the spear as well. Along with this training, he reorganized his legions into groups of 480 men, which would make it easier for Crassus to strategically maneuver the men over the battlefield. By the time these preparations were done, Crassus stood in front of eight well-trained legions. He had full confidence that they would pursue and eradicate Spartacus and his slave army. With this, Crassus marched after Spartacus.

It is possible that after his victory at the Battle of Picenum, Spartacus thought he had seen a difference in the Roman forces. Perhaps he thought that his troops were not ready to take Rome on. However, this is just a theory; it is not known exactly why Spartacus left Rome untouched. Even though he was only kilometers away from the city, he decided to take his troops south, where he continued raiding and plundering the Italian countryside. Eventually, he would take the town of Thurii, and he would treat this city almost as if it was his capital. Spartacus's army then marched into the Lucania region, experiencing many small defeats along the way.

With Crassus hot on his trail, the gladiator general found himself in Bruttium (located in the toe of Italy) and then found his way to Rhegium (a coastal city on the mainland that was not far from Messana—modern-day Messina—on Sicily). Spartacus thought Sicily might be the perfect location to set up a more permanent camp. After all, Sicily had been home to the previous two slave rebellions, so Spartacus likely felt there would be kindred spirits on the island who could help build an even larger army and set Rome ablaze.

But the only way to cross the Strait of Messana (Messina) without utilizing Roman ships was to barter with the Sicilian pirates. Spartacus had some wealth by this point, as he had spent months raiding estates. He was soon able to find some Sicilian pirates and offered to pay them to ferry thousands of men to Sicily. Spartacus, though, would find out the bitter sting of betrayal, as the pirates who had taken the money and agreed to the contract failed to show up at the rendezvous point.

Of course, this left Spartacus and his gladiator army in a very poor position. Crassus acted quickly and reworked his strategy. Instead of facing the large slave army on the battlefield, Crassus opted to build a wall that would corner Spartacus on the peninsula. This wall would allow Crassus to not expend any supplies or men but rather wait for the slave army to be starved into submission.

According to Plutarch, the famed Greek historian, the Roman commander instructed his legions to dig a fifteen-foot-wide ditch across a thirty-five-mile stretch of land. Once that was done, then wood and stone were used to create a wall.

Spartacus was annoyed by the construction of this wall, but he continued looking for another way to get his troops out of this predicament. Afraid that he would be unable to conquer the wall, Spartacus sent word to Crassus that he was ready to enter into peace negotiations. But Crassus took this as a sure sign that his plan was working and rejected the slave general's offer. This left Spartacus back in the same position he was in, and that meant he had to figure out how to overcome the Romans' strategy.

Winter approached rapidly, and Spartacus and his army were running low on supplies. The gladiator general knew that the only way to get out of this predicament was to go through the wall, and for this to happen, he had to devise a strategic plan. Spartacus and his men waited for night to fall on one winter evening, and when the visibility was low due to a winter storm, they stealthily found a small section of the ditch and filled it with wood and earth. After creating a bridge across the ditch, Spartacus and his forces then battered down the wall, freeing themselves from the siege.

The slave army rapidly moved into Lucania, and this move sent waves of panic throughout Rome. Crassus's inability to stop the slave army left the Roman Senate feeling that they needed to bolster the legions already combating this menace. They knew their next decision had to be something big, so they sent word to Pompey and Marcus Terentius Varro Lucullus to return home and join forces with Crassus. This created a sense of urgency in Crassus, as he did not want to share any of the glory with other political rivals, let alone Pompey and Lucullus. Both of these Roman commanders had seen widespread success in several different campaigns. Lucullus had gained quite a reputation through his career; he had been in Macedonia when he was recalled back to Italy. Pompey had done the same with his campaigns in Hispania.

The long winter and the seashore took their toll on the gladiator army, and cracks began to appear within the command. A large band of men chose to splinter from Spartacus and follow two Gallic warriors named Gannicus and Castus. This new faction set up camp in a small area near a lake in Lucania. Hearing word of this dissension, Crassus sent around six thousand men to the location and instructed them to take the high ground. They were to do this before the slaves could do so and to do it quietly so as not to alert their enemies. However, the troops were unable to complete that portion of the mission, as they were seen. Learning of this, Crassus had to act quickly, and he rushed into the battle that had broken out. The battle was furious and fast, but the rebellious slave army stood their ground and held off the Roman soldiers until Spartacus could arrive with reinforcements. Even with these reinforcements, Crassus and his Romans legions were able to slaughter over twelve thousand of the faction's men.

Spartacus and his army retreated toward the area surrounding Petelia, looking to set up a defensive camp in the mountains. Knowing that he had delivered a devastating blow, Crassus sent two of his lieutenants and several legions to pursue Spartacus. Scrophas and Quintus took their men and executed several attacks on the rear flanks of Spartacus's army. Knowing that he would never make it to his planned destination without shaking the legions trailing behind him, Spartacus quickly turned his forces around and attacked the legions head-on. Once again, this strategic move threw the Roman legions off-kilter, and the furious battle ended with the Roman forces being decimated. Many of the Roman legionnaires were cut down in battle. Scrophas was rescued by his men; he barely made it out of the battle alive.

When the slave army heard that reinforcements led by Pompey and Lucullus were arriving, they knew it would make a bad situation even worse. At the same time, though, Spartacus's army was once again energized by the stunning defeat they had just given to the Roman legions. Regardless, Spartacus still felt the best plan of action was to move to the high ground and build a defensive line. However, his generals and his army were unwilling to retreat any farther. Instead, they urged their leader to arm everyone once again and march headlong into the oncoming Roman legions. Some of Spartacus's leaders also felt that the better plan would be to move south to Brundisium, where they could hire a merchant ship and escape the mainland to recollect themselves before attempting another run at Rome. The slaves' uncertainty played right into Crassus's hands, as he wanted to end the conflict before his rivals could reach the region so that he could gain all the glory of taking down Spartacus and the slave rebellion.

But unfortunately, that plan, though sound, would be thwarted by the fact that Lucullus and his legions landed at that very city and began moving inland to meet up with Crassus and his men. Spartacus was trapped between two armies, as well as another approaching one, but he still attempted to refrain from battle as much as possible.

Crassus somehow found his way into close proximity of the gladiator army's camp and prepared for what he deemed would be the final battle. Once again, the Roman commander sent orders to several of his men to begin digging a trench around the slave encampment. The slave army soon caught wind of this, and many of them began jumping into the ditch and attacking the Roman soldiers. As more and more of the slave soldiers sprang to action, Spartacus knew that conflict would not be avoided, and so, choosing the lesser of three evils, he pulled his soldiers together and moved on Crassus.

After having called for battle, Spartacus's men brought him his horse, and in an act of defiance, the gladiator drew his weapon and struck it down. By doing this, he made it clear that there was no other choice but to fight until they had no breath left or until every Roman soldier was under their boot. The mighty slave army rushed forward, outnumbering the Roman legions by many. They ran straight into the legions' wall of shields and experienced swords. Having been repelled initially, Spartacus gathered his troops together once again and advanced forward.

Swords and bodies were falling left and right, and Spartacus was determined to meet the leader of this legion one on one, so he made his way through soldiers and bodies until he saw Crassus across the field, sitting on top of a small hill and watching the battle from a distance. Spirited on by the sight of his rival, Spartacus pushed through, killing legionnaire after legionnaire, but he was never able to make it to the Roman commander himself. Unfortunately for Spartacus, his legend preceded him. When several of the legionaries saw who he was, they turned and encircled him.

Spartacus had been struck several times on his push through the mass of men on his mission to clash swords with Crassus, but even though he had suffered many injuries, the proud Thracian warrior stood his ground. Supposedly, as the Roman legionnaires swarmed upon him, he continued fighting until the last breath left his body. (It should be noted, though, that his body was never recovered, but most historians assume he died in this battle.)

Crassus had done what no other Roman general and commander had been able to do. He had completely annihilated the bulk of the gladiator army. Though many of Spartacus's men fled the battle and found refuge in the hills, the bulk of his forces were wiped out. However, Crassus had also taken quite a beating, which means it was up to the other Roman commanders to track down the remaining fugitive slaves.

Pompey used this to elevate his role in the annihilation of the slave army by routing as many of the slaves as possible. Pompey, Crassus, and Lucullus killed or captured over ten thousand slaves. Now all that was left for Crassus and his legions was to triumphantly return to Rome along the Appian Way. This road was an ancient route that had been used to transport military supplies since 312 BCE. Taking this road into the capital not only made the march easier but also made a statement. As Crassus and the other generals marched along the Appian Way, they would be visible by many people. This allowed the victorious commander to send a message to the remaining slaves and lower-class Roman citizens as he traveled to Rome.

Crassus supposedly captured six thousand slaves, who he crucified on the road to Rome. The Roman commander would stop every few feet and order his men to mount a slave and raise them high above the ground. The slaves, who were writhing in pain upon the cross, could be heard for great distances and were left to die so that anyone traveling down the main road into Rome would know what would happen if they dared to stand up or rebel against the Roman Republic. This decisive victory and subsequent punishments ended the Third Servile War and showed many the might of the Roman Republic.

Conclusion

Though undoubtedly every one of the Servile Wars played a part in changing the Roman Republic, the third one may have had the most impact. Without the First and Second Servile Wars, though, there is no telling if the slaves of that gladiator school would have had the courage to stand up and fight.

Sicily was greatly changed by the consequences of the Servile Wars. The Romans realized they had to have a larger presence on the island, so the Roman government opted to increase the urbanization of several of the major cities. This allowed them to have a bigger hold on the island and, therefore, on the slaves within its borders.

Since the Third Servile War took place on the mainland and hit so close to home for the Roman elite, many of whom lived in the capital, it had more of an impact than the other two insurrections. It was the largest of the slave revolts, and it was led by men who were mighty enough to stand up against some of the most well-decorated geniuses of the Roman military. The defeat of Spartacus and his slave army would elevate names like Crassus and Pompey to new heights.

Although Pompey was not involved in the final battle itself, the fact that his legions were able to capture so many of the fleeing warrior slaves would bring him new avenues of power. The actions of Pompey would also create tensions with Crassus and build a lifelong rivalry. Pompey's decision to claim credit for ending the war didn't sit well with Crassus or his supporters.

Though their rivalry was ignited through this conflict, both Pompey and Crassus received a hero's welcome when they returned home to Rome with their men. The two generals wouldn't enter Rome itself. Instead, they chose to keep their legions intact and set up camp on the outskirts of the capital. Their victory against Spartacus allowed them to be put up for consulship in 70 BCE, despite the fact that Pompey was not even eligible for this position due to his age (he was only thirty-five). But because of the mighty victory these two generals had delivered, the Roman Senate elected both as consuls. However, there is some speculation on if the presence of their men outside of the city walls aided them in their political win.

Not only did Spartacus's war affect the political lives of the two men who were able to bring the gladiator to his knees, but it also affected the lands ripped apart by the conflict. Like with the other two Servile Wars, the Third Servile War devastated southern Italy. Towns were razed to the ground, and many of the slaves of these towns and estates, along with the poorer classes, had laid down their tools and picked up weapons in hopes of freedom. This left many of the slaves who were able to escape into the wilderness without any means of survival. Looking for food and money to survive, many of these slaves turned to crime, which left southern Italy rife with bands of criminals.

Economically, the uprising by Spartacus and the subsequent war left many southern Italian landowners struggling financially with properties that either had been completely destroyed or damaged. It took years for them to find their footing again. All of this devastation left the latifundia system of southern Italy in total disarray. These parcels of land that had been once gained through the conquering of local tribes had become privately owned parcels of land that were passed down in families. These estates often raised livestock or cultivated olive oil and wine. Most of these were owned by wealthy

Roman elites, but with the new atmosphere of the republic caused by the slave revolts, these upper-class Roman citizens had to come up with a new system.

With the slave shortage, these estate owners chose to find a way to maintain their lands without using slaves. The answer to this problem was renting out portions of their land to individuals who would work it and take care of the livestock. For this, the estate owners would be given rent and a share of the crops, much like the feudal system that would be present in medieval Europe. Even with the shortage of slaves, there were many landowners who still utilized a small group of slaves to ensure that household chores and other menial labor were completed.

Of course, with this change of work distribution, the Roman elite also had to figure out a new way to ensure their slaves were kept under control. This sometimes led to minor rebellious uprisings on individual estates. This is why during this transitional period, it was common to see search parties out in the Italian countryside looking for escaped slaves.

For the most part, though, these estate owners began using fewer and fewer slaves and instead offered a small wage to freemen in order to ensure that all of their crops were maintained and harvested. Overall, many Romans' views on slaves themselves were altered with the rise of Spartacus. After all, Spartacus had been a slave and yet had had many of the attributes and virtues that Roman citizens held in high regard. On top of this, the Roman emperors who followed in the coming centuries concentrated more on building the empire they had rather than expanding it any further. This meant a decreased influx of slaves, which left estate owners having to look at hiring laborers rather than purchasing slaves who had been captured.

This new outlook and the shortage of slaves also impacted the legal rights of those still held as slaves. Beginning with Emperor Claudius, new laws were put in place during the Roman Empire that elevated the protection of slaves. The first of these laws to be enacted stated that any slave owner who murdered an elderly or sickly slave would be charged with murder. This law also stated that if an elderly or sickly slave was not provided any assistance, they automatically earned freedom. More laws were to come that would increase the rights of slaves. Many of these built upon the idea that slave owners would be held responsible for the mistreatment and murder of their slaves.

For centuries after the Third Servile War, laws on slaves began to change and expand. Many historians and experts agree that the conflict and the subsequent devastation of the lands that came about definitely played a part in igniting the flame of more rights for slaves. Though the extent of this may never be known, there was a marked decrease in slave ownership in the Roman Empire. On top of this, the perception of slavery began changing drastically, and the Roman leaders and elites worked hard to ensure that such an uprising never happened again. In fact, the Third Servile War not only was the largest of the slave uprisings, but it was also the last major one in both the Roman Republic and Roman Empire.

Here's another book by Captivating History that you might like

SPARTACUS

A CAPTIVATING GUIDE TO THE THRACIAN GLADIATOR WHO LED THE SLAVE REBELLION CALLED THE THIRD SERVILE WAR AGAINST THE ROMAN REPUBLIC

CAPTIVATING HISTORY

Free Bonus from Captivating History (Available for a Limited time)

Hi History Lovers!

Now you have a chance to join our exclusive history list so you can get your first history ebook for free as well as discounts and a potential to get more history books for free! Simply visit the link below to join.

Captivatinghistory.com/ebook

Also, make sure to follow us on Facebook, Twitter and Youtube by searching for Captivating History.

References

Bradley, Keith, Professor; Resisting Slavery in Ancient Rome (February 2011) Retrieved from http://www.bbc.co.uk/history/ancient/romans/slavery_01.shtml

Salem Media; Ancient Roman Slaves: A Life of Bondage (September 2021) Retrieved from https://www.historyonthenet.com/ancient-roman-slaves

Garland, Robert Ph.D.; Roman Slavery: Who Were the Roman Slaves? (December 2020) Retrieved from https://www.thegreatcoursesdaily.com/roman-slavery-who-were-the-roman-slaves/

Cartwright, Mark; Slavery in the Roman World (November 2013) Retrieved from https://www.worldhistory.org/article/629/slavery-in-the-roman-world/

Wikipedia; Slavery in Ancient Rome (August 2021) Retrieved from https://en.wikipedia.org/wiki/Slavery_in_ancient_Rome

Wikipedia; First Servile War (September 2021) Retrieved from https://en.wikipedia.org/wiki/First_Servile_War

Military Wiki; First Servile War; Retrieved from https://military.wikia.org/wiki/First_Servile_War

History Wiki; First Servile War; Retrieved from https://historica.fandom.com/wiki/First_Servile_War

Academic Kids; First Servile War; Retrieved from http://academickids.com/encyclopedia/index.php/First_Servile_War

Gill, N. S.; The Sicilian Revolts of Enslaved Persons and Spartacus (September 2018) Retrieved from https://www.thoughtco.com/slave-revolts-or-servile-wars-in-italy-112744

Heritagedaily; Eunus – The Roman Slave Who Declared Himself King (July 2021) Retrieved from https://www.heritagedaily.com/2021/07/eunus-the-roman-slave-who-declared-himself-king/139690

Encyclopedia Britannica Editors; Eunus – Roman Slave (November 2019) Retrieved from https://www.britannica.com/biography/Eunus

Wikipedia; Sicilian Wars (August 2021) Retrieved from https://en.wikipedia.org/wiki/Sicilian_Wars

Wikipedia; Battle of Himera (July 2021) Retrieved from https://en.wikipedia.org/wiki/Battle_of_Himera_(480_BC)

Wikipedia; Treaty of Lutatius (June 2021) Retrieved from https://en.wikipedia.org/wiki/Treaty_of_Lutatius

Wikipedia; Battle of Selinus (August 2021) Retrieved from https://en.wikipedia.org/wiki/Battle_of_Selinus

Wikipedia; Siege of Akragas (July 2021) Retrieved from https://en.wikipedia.org/wiki/Siege_of_Akragas_(406_BC)

Wikipedia; Cleon (June 2021) Retrieved from https://en.wikipedia.org/wiki/Cleon_(revolted_slave)

Author Unknown; The First Slave Revolt Was Led by Eunus; Retrieved from https://www.the-romans.eu/slavery/Slave-revolt.php

Wiedeman, Thomas; Greek and Roman Slavery (1981) Retrieved from http://www.professorcampbell.org/sources/slavewar.html

Barca, Natale; Rome's Sicilian Slave Wars: The Revolts of Eunus and Salvius, 136-132 and 105-100BC (August 2020) Published by Pen and Sword Military

Livius, Titus; The History of Rome; Retrieved from http://www.perseus.tufts.edu/hopper/text?doc=Perseus%3Atext%3A1999.02.0150%3Abook%3D68

Wikipedia; Cimbri (September 2021) Retrieved from https://en.wikipedia.org/wiki/Cimbri

Tsouras, Peter; The Cimbrian War, 113-101 B.C. (March 2014) Retrieved from https://www.historynet.com/cimbrian-war-113-101-b-c.htm

Hughes, Tristan; How Gaius Marius Saved Rome from the Cimbri (February 2020) Retrieved from https://www.historyhit.com/how-gaius-marius-saved-rome-from-the-cimbri/

Wikipedia; Cimbrian War (August 2021) Retrieved from https://en.wikipedia.org/wiki/Cimbrian_War

Wikipedia; Second Servile War (August 2021) Retrieved from https://en.wikipedia.org/wiki/Second_Servile_War#Athenion

Siculus, Diodorus; Book 36; Retrieved from http://attalus.org/translate/diodorus36.html

Wikipedia; Lucius Licinius Lucullus (September 2021) Retrieved from https://en.wikipedia.org/wiki/Lucius_Licinius_Lucullus_(praetor_104_BC)

Wikipedia; Battle of the Silarius River (August 2021) Retrieved from https://en.wikipedia.org/wiki/Battle_of_the_Silarius_River

Wikipedia; Battle of Picenum (May 2021) Retrieved from https://en.wikipedia.org/wiki/Battle_of_Picenum

Wikipedia; Battle of Mount Vesuvius (February 2021) Retrieved from https://en.wikipedia.org/wiki/Battle_of_Mount_Vesuvius

Wikipedia; Battle of Cantenna (July 2021) Retrieved from https://en.wikipedia.org/wiki/Battle_of_Cantenna

UKEssays; Spartacus and the Slave Rebellion in Rome, History Essay (November 2018) Retrieved from https://www.ukessays.com/essays/history/spartacus-and-the-slave-rebellion-in-rome-history-essay.php

Author Unknown; Rome's Third Servile War: One of the First Great Battles Against Slavery (September 2019) Retrieved from https://worldhistory.us/ancient-history/ancient-rome/romes-third-servile-war-one-of-the-first-great-battles-against-slavery.php

Czech, Kenneth P.; Spartacus, The Grecian Slave Warrior Who Threatened Rome (April 1994) Retrieved from https://www.historynet.com/spartacus-the-grecian-slave-warrior-who-threatened-rome.htm

S., Alen; Third Servile War in Roman Republic 73-71 BCE (Spartacus Rebellion) (April 2016) Retrieved from https://www.shorthistory.org/ancient-civilizations/ancient-rome/third-servile-war-in-roman-republic-73-71bc-spartacus-rebellion/

Mark, Joshua J.; The Spartacus Revolt (March 2016) Retrieved from https://www.worldhistory.org/article/871/the-spartacus-revolt/

Encyclopedia Britannica Editors; Third Servile War; Retrieved from https://www.britannica.com/event/Gladiatorial-War

Wikipedia; Third Servile War (August 2021) Retrieved from https://en.wikipedia.org/wiki/Third_Servile_War

Russell; Gladiators of Ancient Rome (February 2011) Retrieved from https://www.carpediemrome.com/gladiators-in-ancient-rome/

Gill, N. S.; Roman Gladiators: A Dangerous Job for a Chance for a Better Life (October 2019) Retrieved from https://www.thoughtco.com/roman-gladiators-overview-120901

Wikipedia; Gladiator (August 2021) Retrieved from https://en.wikipedia.org/wiki/Gladiator

Daily History Editors; What Was the Impact of Spartacus' Uprising on Rome (January 2019) Retrieved from https://dailyhistory.org/What_was_the_impact_of_Spartacus'_uprising_on_Rome

Wikipedia; Spartacus (October 2021) Retrieved from https://en.wikipedia.org/wiki/Spartacus

Yourdictionary; Spartacus; Retrieved from https://biography.yourdictionary.com/spartacus

Unknown Author; Spartacus; Retrieved from https://www.livius.org/articles/person/spartacus/

Jarus, Owen; Spartacus: History of Gladiator Revolt Leader (September 2013) Retrieved from https://www.livescience.com/39730-spartacus.html

Wikipedia; Crixus (May 2021) Retrieved from https://en.wikipedia.org/wiki/Crixus

Dimuro, Gina; Crixus: Spartacus' Right-Hand Man Who May Have Been the Gladiator Army's Downfall (January 2019) Retrieved from https://allthatsinteresting.com/crixus

Wikipedia; Oenomaus (September 2021) Retrieved from https://en.wikipedia.org/wiki/Oenomaus_(rebel_slave)

Livius.org; Plutarch on Spartacus; Retrieved from https://www.livius.org/sources/content/plutarch/plutarchs-crassus/plutarch-on-spartacus/

White, Horace; Appian, The Civil Wars; Retrieved from http://www.perseus.tufts.edu/hopper/text?doc=Perseus:abo:tlg,0551,017:1:14

Wikipedia; Publius Varinius (July 2021) Retrieved from https://en.wikipedia.org/wiki/Publius_Varinius

Wikipedia; Lucius Gellius (March 2021) Retrieved from https://en.wikipedia.org/wiki/Lucius_Gellius

Wikipedia; Gnaeus Cornelius Lentulus Clodianus (August 2021) Retrieved from https://en.wikipedia.org/wiki/Gnaeus_Cornelius_Lentulus_Clodianus

Williams, Julie; The Third Servile War Timeline (April 2016) Retrieved from https://prezi.com/fhto4b5qjrvn/the-third-servile-war-timeline/

Wikipedia; Quintus Arrius (November 2020) Retrieved from https://en.wikipedia.org/wiki/Quintus_Arrius_(praetor_73_BC)

Wikipedia; Marcus Licinius Crassus (October 2021) Retrieved from https://en.wikipedia.org/wiki/Marcus_Licinius_Crassus

Wikipedia; Pompey (October 2021) Retrieved from https://en.wikipedia.org/wiki/Pompey

Wikipedia; Appian Way (October 2021) Retrieved from https://en.wikipedia.org/wiki/Appian_Way

Schools Wikipedia; History of Slavery (2007) Retrieved from https://www.cs.mcgill.ca/~rwest/wikispeedia/wpcd/wp/h/History_of_slavery.htm

Wikipedia; Slavery in Antiquity (August 2021) Retrieved from https://en.wikipedia.org/wiki/Slavery_in_antiquity

Printed in Great Britain
by Amazon

TABLE OF CONTENTS

T&P Books' Theme-Based Dictionaries	4
Pronunciation guide	11
Abbreviations	13

BASIC CONCEPTS   14

1. Pronouns	14
2. Greetings. Salutations	14
3. Questions	15
4. Prepositions	15
5. Function words. Adverbs. Part 1	16
6. Function words. Adverbs. Part 2	18

NUMBERS. MISCELLANEOUS   19

7. Cardinal numbers. Part 1	19
8. Cardinal numbers. Part 2	20
9. Ordinal numbers	20

COLOURS. UNITS OF MEASUREMENT   22

10. Colors	22
11. Units of measurement	23
12. Containers	24

MAIN VERBS   25

13. The most important verbs. Part 1	25
14. The most important verbs. Part 2	26
15. The most important verbs. Part 3	26
16. The most important verbs. Part 4	28

TIME. CALENDAR   29

17. Weekdays	29
18. Hours. Day and night	29
19. Months. Seasons	30

TRAVEL. HOTEL 33

20. Trip. Travel 33
21. Hotel 34
22. Sightseeing 34

TRANSPORTATION 36

23. Airport 36
24. Airplane 37
25. Train 38
26. Ship 39

CITY 41

27. Urban transportation 41
28. City. Life in the city 42
29. Urban institutions 43
30. Signs 44
31. Shopping 46

CLOTHING & ACCESSORIES 47

32. Outerwear. Coats 47
33. Men's & women's clothing 47
34. Clothing. Underwear 48
35. Headwear 48
36. Footwear 48
37. Personal accessories 49
38. Clothing. Miscellaneous 49
39. Personal care. Cosmetics 50
40. Watches. Clocks 51

EVERYDAY EXPERIENCE 52

41. Money 52
42. Post. Postal service 53
43. Banking 54
44. Telephone. Phone conversation 55
45. Mobile telephone 55
46. Stationery 56
47. Foreign languages 56

MEALS. RESTAURANT 58

48. Table setting 58

49. Restaurant	58
50. Meals	59
51. Cooked dishes	59
52. Food	60
53. Drinks	62
54. Vegetables	63
55. Fruits. Nuts	64
56. Bread. Candy	65
57. Spices	65

PERSONAL INFORMATION. FAMILY 67

58. Personal information. Forms	67
59. Family members. Relatives	67
60. Friends. Coworkers	68

HUMAN BODY. MEDICINE 70

61. Head	70
62. Human body	71
63. Diseases	72
64. Symptoms. Treatments. Part 1	73
65. Symptoms. Treatments. Part 2	74
66. Symptoms. Treatments. Part 3	75
67. Medicine. Drugs. Accessories	76

APARTMENT 77

68. Apartment	77
69. Furniture. Interior	77
70. Bedding	78
71. Kitchen	78
72. Bathroom	79
73. Household appliances	80

THE EARTH. WEATHER 82

74. Outer space	82
75. The Earth	83
76. Cardinal directions	84
77. Sea. Ocean	84
78. Seas' and Oceans' names	85
79. Mountains	86
80. Mountains names	87
81. Rivers	87
82. Rivers' names	88
83. Forest	89

84.	Natural resources	90
85.	Weather	91
86.	Severe weather. Natural disasters	92

FAUNA 93

87.	Mammals. Predators	93
88.	Wild animals	93
89.	Domestic animals	95
90.	Birds	96
91.	Fish. Marine animals	97
92.	Amphibians. Reptiles	98
93.	Insects	98

FLORA 100

94.	Trees	100
95.	Shrubs	101
96.	Fruits. Berries	101
97.	Flowers. Plants	102
98.	Cereals, grains	103

COUNTRIES OF THE WORLD 104

99.	Countries. Part 1	104
100.	Countries. Part 2	105
101.	Countries. Part 3	106

PRONUNCIATION GUIDE

Letter	Turkish example	T&P phonetic alphabet	English example

Vowels

Letter	Turkish example	T&P phonetic alphabet	English example
A a	ada	[a]	shorter than in ask
E e	eş	[e]	elm, medal
I ı	tıp	[ı]	big, America
İ i	isim	[i]	shorter than in feet
O o	top	[ɔ]	bottle, doctor
Ö ö	ödül	[ø]	eternal, church
U u	mum	[u]	book
Ü ü	süt	[y]	fuel, tuna

Consonants

Letter	Turkish example	T&P phonetic alphabet	English example
B b	baba	[b]	baby, book
C c	cam	[ʤ]	joke, general
Ç ç	çay	[ʧ]	church, French
D d	diş	[d]	day, doctor
F f	fikir	[f]	face, food
G g	güzel	[g]	game, gold
Ğ ğ [1]	oğul		no sound
Ğ ğ [2]	öğle vakti	[j]	yes, New York
H h	hata	[h]	home, have
J j	jest	[ʒ]	forge, pleasure
K k	komşu	[k]	clock, kiss
L l	lise	[l]	lace, people
M m	meydan	[m]	magic, milk
N n	neşe	[n]	name, normal
P p	posta	[p]	pencil, private
R r	rakam	[r]	rice, radio
S s	sabah	[s]	city, boss
Ş ş	şarkı	[ʃ]	machine, shark
T t	tren	[t]	tourist, trip

Letter	Turkish example	T&P phonetic alphabet	English example
V v	vazo	[v]	very, river
Y y	yaş	[j]	yes, New York
Z z	zil	[z]	zebra, please

Comments

* Letters Ww, Xx used in foreign words only
1 silent after hard vowels (a, ı, o, u) and lengthens this vowel
2 after soft vowels (e, i, ö, ü)

ABBREVIATIONS
used in the vocabulary

ab.	-	about
adj	-	adjective
adv	-	adverb
anim.	-	animate
as adj	-	attributive noun used as adjective
e.g.	-	for example
etc.	-	et cetera
fam.	-	familiar
fem.	-	feminine
form.	-	formal
inanim.	-	inanimate
masc.	-	masculine
math	-	mathematics
mil.	-	military
n	-	noun
pl	-	plural
pron.	-	pronoun
sb	-	somebody
sing.	-	singular
sth	-	something
v aux	-	auxiliary verb
vi	-	intransitive verb
vi, vt	-	intransitive, transitive verb
vt	-	transitive verb

BASIC CONCEPTS

1. Pronouns

I, me	ben	[bæn]
you	sen	[sæn]
he, she, it	o	[o]
we	biz	[biz]
you (to a group)	siz	[siz]
they	onlar	[onlar]

2. Greetings. Salutations

Hello! (fam.)	Selam!	[sæʎam]
Hello! (form.)	Merhaba!	[mærhaba]
Good morning!	Günaydın!	[gynajdın]
Good afternoon!	İyi günler!	[ijı gynlær]
Good evening!	İyi akşamlar!	[ijı akʃamlar]
to say hello	selam vermek	[sæʎam værmæk]
Hi! (hello)	Selam!, Merhaba!	[sæʎam mærhaba]
greeting (n)	selam	[sæʎam]
to greet (vt)	selamlamak	[sæʎamlamak]
How are you?	Nasılsın?	[nasılsın]
What's new?	Ne var ne yok?	[næ var næ jok]
Bye-Bye! Goodbye!	Hoşca kalın!	[hoʃʤa kalın]
See you soon!	Görüşürüz!	[gøryʃyryz]
Farewell! (to a friend)	Güle güle!	[gylæ gylæ]
Farewell (form.)	Elveda!	[æʎvæda]
to say goodbye	vedalaşmak	[vædalaʃmak]
So long!	Hoşça kal!	[hoʃtʃa kal]
Thank you!	Teşekkür ederim!	[tæʃækkyr ædærim]
Thank you very much!	Çok teşekkür ederim!	[tʃok tæʃækkyr ædærim]
You're welcome	Rica ederim	[ridʒa ædærim]
Don't mention it!	Bir şey değil	[bir ʃæj di:ʎ]
It was nothing	Estağfurullah	[æsta:furulla]
Excuse me! (fam.)	Affedersin!	[afædærsin]
Excuse me! (form.)	Affedersiniz!	[afædærsiniz]
to excuse (forgive)	affetmek	[afætmæk]
to apologize (vi)	özür dilemek	[øzyr dilæmæk]

My apologies	Özür dilerim	[øzyr dilærim]
I'm sorry!	Affedersiniz!	[afædærsiniz]
to forgive (vt)	affetmek	[afætmæk]
please (adv)	lütfen	[lytfæn]

Don't forget!	Unutmayın!	[unutmajın]
Certainly!	Kesinlikle!	[kæsinliktæ]
Of course not!	Tabi ki hayır!	[tabi ki hajır]
Okay! (I agree)	Tamam!	[tamam]
That's enough!	Yeter artık!	[jætær artık]

3. Questions

Who?	Kim?	[kim]
What?	Ne?	[næ]
Where? (at, in)	Nerede?	[nærædæ]
Where (to)?	Nereye?	[næræjæ]
From where?	Nereden?	[nærædæn]
When?	Ne zaman?	[næ zaman]
Why? (What for?)	Neden?	[nædæn]
Why? (reason)	Neden?	[nædæn]

What for?	Ne için?	[næ itʃin]
How? (in what way)	Nasıl?	[nasıl]
What? (What kind of ...?)	Hangi?	[haŋi]
Which?	Kaçıncı?	[katʃindʒı]

To whom?	Kime?	[kimæ]
About whom?	Kim hakkında?	[kim hakında]
About what?	Ne hakkında?	[næ hakkında]
With whom?	Kimle?	[kimlæ]

How many?	Ne kadar?	[næ kadar]
How much?	Kaç?	[katʃ]
Whose?	Kimin?	[kimin]

4. Prepositions

with (accompanied by)	... -ile, ... -le, ... -la	[ilæ], [læ], [la]
without	... -sız, ... -suz	[sız], [suz]
to (indicating direction)	... -e, ... -a	[æ], [a]
about (talking ~ ...)	hakkında	[hakkında]
before (in time)	önce	[øndʒæ]
in front of ...	önünde	[ønyndæ]

under (beneath, below)	altında	[altında]
above (over)	üstünde	[justyndæ]
on (atop)	üstüne	[justynæ]

from (off, out of)	... -den, ... -dan	[dæn], [dan]
of (made from)	... -den, ... -dan	[dæn], [dan]
in (e.g., ~ ten minutes)	sonra	[sonra]
over (across the top of)	üstünden	[justyndæn]

5. Function words. Adverbs. Part 1

Where? (at, in)	Nerede?	[næræedæ]
here (adv)	burada	[burada]
there (adv)	orada	[orada]
somewhere (to be)	bir yerde	[birʲ jærdæ]
nowhere (not anywhere)	hiç bir yerde	[hitʃ birʲ jærdæ]
by (near, beside)	... yanında	[janında]
by the window	pencerenin yanında	[pændʒærænin janında]
Where (to)?	Nereye?	[næræjæ]
here (e.g., come ~!)	buraya	[buraja]
there (e.g., to go ~)	oraya	[oraja]
from here (adv)	buradan	[buradan]
from there (adv)	oradan	[oradan]
close (adv)	yakında	[jakında]
far (adv)	uzağa	[uza:]
near (e.g., ~ Paris)	yakında	[jakında]
nearby (adv)	yakınında	[jakınında]
not far (adv)	civarında	[dʒivarında]
left (adj)	sol	[sol]
on the left	solda	[solda]
to the left	sola	[sola]
right (adj)	sağ	[sa:]
on the right	sağda	[sa:da]
to the right	sağa	[sa:]
in front (adv)	önde	[øndæ]
front (as adj)	ön	[øn]
ahead (look ~)	ileri	[ilæri]
behind (adv)	arkada	[arkada]
from behind	arkadan	[arkadan]
back (towards the rear)	geriye	[gærijæ]
middle	orta	[orta]
in the middle	ortasında	[ortasında]
at the side	kenarda	[kænarda]

PLAY MONEY

| everywhere (adv) | her yerde | [hær jærdæ] |
| around (in all directions) | çevrede | [tʃævrædæ] |

from inside	içeriden	[itʃæridæn]
somewhere (to go)	bir yere	[bir jæræ]
straight (directly)	dosdoğru	[dosdo:ru]
back (e.g., come ~)	geri	[gæri]

| from anywhere | bir yerden | [bir jærdæn] |
| from somewhere | bir yerden | [bir jærdæn] |

firstly (adv)	ilk olarak	[iʎk olarak]
secondly (adv)	ikinci olarak	[ikindʒi olarak]
thirdly (adv)	üçüncü olarak	[jutʃundʒy olarak]

suddenly (adv)	birdenbire	[birdænbiræ]
at first (adv)	başlangıçta	[baʃlaŋıtʃta]
for the first time	ilk kez	[ilk kæz]
long before ...	çok daha önce ...	[tʃok da: øndʒæ]
anew (over again)	yeniden	[jænidæn]
for good (adv)	sonsuza kadar	[sonsuza kadar]

never (adv)	hiçbir zaman	[hitʃbir zaman]
again (adv)	tekrar	[tækrar]
now (adv)	şimdi	[ʃimdi]
often (adv)	sık	[sık]
then (adv)	o zaman	[o zaman]
urgently (quickly)	acele	[adʒælæ]
usually (adv)	genellikle	[gænælliklæ]

by the way, ...	aklıma gelmişken, ...	[aklıma gæʎmiʃkæn]
possible (that is ~)	mümkündür	[mymkyndyr]
probably (adv)	muhtemelen	[muhtæmælæn]
maybe (adv)	olabilir	[olabilir]
besides ...	ayrıca ...	[ajrıdʒa]
that's why ...	onun için	[onun itʃin]
in spite of ...	rağmen ...	[ra:mæn]
thanks to ...	... sayesinde	[sajæsindæ]

what (pron.)	ne	[næ]
that (conj.)	... -ki, ... -dığı, ... -diği	[ki], [dı:], [di:]
something	bir şey	[bir ʃæj]
anything (something)	bir şey	[bir ʃæj]
nothing	hiçbir şey	[hitʃbir ʃæj]

who (pron.)	kim	[kim]
someone	birisi	[birisı]
somebody	birisi	[birisı]

nobody	hiç kimse	[hitʃ kimsæ]
nowhere (a voyage to ~)	hiçbir yere	[hitʃbir jæræ]
nobody's	kimsesiz	[kimsæsiz]

somebody's	birinin	[birinin]
so (I'm ~ glad)	öylesine	[øjlæsinæ]
also (as well)	dahi, ayrıca	[dahi], [ajrıdʒa]
too (as well)	da	[da]

6. Function words. Adverbs. Part 2

Why?	Neden?	[nædæn]
for some reason	nedense	[nædænsæ]
because ...	çünkü	[tʃuŋkju]
for some purpose	her nedense	[hær nædænsæ]

and	ve	[væ]
or	veya	[væja]
but	fakat	[fakat]
for (e.g., ~ me)	için	[itʃin]

too (~ many people)	fazla	[fazla]
only (exclusively)	ancak	[andʒak]
exactly (adv)	tam	[tam]
about (more or less)	yaklaşık	[jaklaʃık]

approximately (adv)	yaklaşık olarak	[jaklaʃık olarak]
approximate (adj)	yaklaşık	[jaklaʃık]
almost (adv)	hemen	[hæmæn]
the rest	geri kalan	[gæri kalan]

each (adj)	her biri	[hær biri]
any (no matter which)	herhangi biri	[hærhaŋi biri]
many, much (a lot of)	çok	[tʃok]
many people	birçokları	[birtʃokları]
all (everyone)	hepsi, herkes	[hæpsi], [hærkæz]

in return for ...	... karşılık olarak	[karʃilik olarak]
in exchange (adv)	yerine	[jærinæ]
by hand (made)	elle, el ile	[ællæ], [æʎ ilæ]
hardly (negative opinion)	şüpheli	[ʃyphæli]

probably (adv)	galiba	[galiba]
on purpose (adv)	mahsus	[mahsus]
by accident (adv)	tesadüfen	[tæsadyfæn]

very (adv)	pek	[pæk]
for example (adv)	mesela	[mæsæʎa]
between	arasında	[arasında]
among	ortasında	[ortasında]
so much (such a lot)	kadar	[kadar]
especially (adv)	özellikle	[øzæʎiklæ]

NUMBERS. MISCELLANEOUS

7. Cardinal numbers. Part 1

0 zero	sıfır	[sıfır]
1 one	bir	[bir]
2 two	iki	[iki]
3 three	üç	[juʧ]
4 four	dört	[dørt]
5 five	beş	[bæʃ]
6 six	altı	[altı]
7 seven	yedi	[jædi]
8 eight	sekiz	[sækiz]
9 nine	dokuz	[dokuz]
10 ten	on	[on]
11 eleven	on bir	[on bir]
12 twelve	on iki	[on iki]
13 thirteen	on üç	[on juʧ]
14 fourteen	on dört	[on dørt]
15 fifteen	on beş	[on bæʃ]
16 sixteen	on altı	[on altı]
17 seventeen	on yedi	[on jædi]
18 eighteen	on sekiz	[on sækiz]
19 nineteen	on dokuz	[on dokuz]
20 twenty	yirmi	[jırmi]
21 twenty-one	yirmi bir	[jırmi bir]
22 twenty-two	yirmi iki	[jırmi iki]
23 twenty-three	yirmi üç	[jırmi juʧ]
30 thirty	otuz	[otuz]
31 thirty-one	otuz bir	[otuz bir]
32 thirty-two	otuz iki	[otuz iki]
33 thirty-three	otuz üç	[otuz juʧ]
40 forty	kırk	[kırk]
41 forty-one	kırk bir	[kırk bir]
42 forty-two	kırk iki	[kırk iki]
43 forty-three	kırk üç	[kırk juʧ]
50 fifty	elli	[ælli]
51 fifty-one	elli bir	[ælli bir]
52 fifty-two	elli iki	[ælli iki]

53 fifty-three	elli üç	[ælli juʧ]
60 sixty	altmış	[altmıʃ]
61 sixty-one	altmış bir	[altmıʃ bir]
62 sixty-two	altmış iki	[altmıʃ iki]
63 sixty-three	altmış üç	[altmıʃ juʧ]
70 seventy	yetmiş	[jætmiʃ]
71 seventy-one	yetmiş bir	[jætmiʃ bir]
72 seventy-two	yetmiş iki	[jætmiʃ iki]
73 seventy-three	yetmiş üç	[jætmiʃ juʧ]
80 eighty	seksen	[sæksæn]
81 eighty-one	seksen bir	[sæksæn bir]
82 eighty-two	seksen iki	[sæksæn iki]
83 eighty-three	seksen üç	[sæksæn juʧ]
90 ninety	doksan	[doksan]
91 ninety-one	doksan bir	[doksan bir]
92 ninety-two	doksan iki	[doksan iki]
93 ninety-three	doksan üç	[doksan juʧ]

8. Cardinal numbers. Part 2

100 one hundred	yüz	[juz]
200 two hundred	iki yüz	[iki juz]
300 three hundred	üç yüz	[uʧ juz]
400 four hundred	dört yüz	[dørt juz]
500 five hundred	beş yüz	[bæʃ juz]
600 six hundred	altı yüz	[altı juz]
700 seven hundred	yedi yüz	[jædi juz]
800 eight hundred	sekiz yüz	[sækiz juz]
900 nine hundred	dokuz yüz	[dokuz juz]
1000 one thousand	bin	[bin]
2000 two thousand	iki bin	[iki bin]
3000 three thousand	üç bin	[juʧ bin]
10000 ten thousand	on bin	[on bin]
one hundred thousand	yüz bin	[juz bin]
million	milyon	[bir miʎon]
billion	milyar	[bir miʎjar]

9. Ordinal numbers

first (adj)	birinci	[birindʒi]
second (adj)	ikinci	[ikindʒi]
third (adj)	üçüncü	[uʧundʒy]
fourth (adj)	dördüncü	[dørdyndʒy]

fifth (adj)	**beşinci**	[bæʃindʒi]
sixth (adj)	**altıncı**	[altındʒı]
seventh (adj)	**yedinci**	[jædindʒi]
eighth (adj)	**sekizinci**	[sækizindʒi]
ninth (adj)	**dokuzuncu**	[dokuzundʒu]
tenth (adj)	**onuncu**	[onundʒu]

COLOURS. UNITS OF MEASUREMENT

10. Colors

color	renk	[ræŋk]
shade (tint)	renk tonu	[ræŋk tonu]
hue	renk tonu	[ræŋk tonu]
rainbow	gökkuşağı	[gøkkuʃaɪ]
white (adj)	beyaz	[bæjaz]
black (adj)	siyah	[sijah]
gray (adj)	gri	[gri]
green (adj)	yeşil	[jæʃiʎ]
yellow (adj)	sarı	[sarı]
red (adj)	kırmızı	[kırmızı]
blue (adj)	mavi	[mavi]
light blue (adj)	açık mavi	[atʃık mavi]
pink (adj)	pembe	[pæmbæ]
orange (adj)	turuncu	[turundʒu]
violet (adj)	mor	[mor]
brown (adj)	kahve rengi	[kahvæ ræŋi]
golden (adj)	altın	[altın]
silvery (adj)	gümüşü	[gymyʃy]
beige (adj)	bej rengi	[bæʒ ræŋi]
cream (adj)	krem rengi	[kræm ræŋi]
turquoise (adj)	turkuaz	[turkuaz]
cherry red (adj)	vişne rengi	[viʃnæ ræŋi]
lilac (adj)	leylak rengi	[læjlak ræŋi]
crimson (adj)	koyu kırmızı	[koju kırmızı]
light (adj)	açık	[atʃık]
dark (adj)	koyu	[koju]
bright, vivid (adj)	parlak	[parlak]
colored (pencils)	renkli	[ræŋkli]
color (e.g., ~ film)	renkli	[ræŋkli]
black-and-white (adj)	siyah-beyaz	[sijahbæjaz]
plain (one-colored)	tek renkli	[tæk ræŋkli]
multicolored (adj)	rengârenk	[ræŋjaræŋk]

11. Units of measurement

weight	ağırlık	[aırlık]
length	uzunluk	[uzunluk]
width	en, genişlik	[æn], [gæniʃlik]
height	yükseklik	[juksæklik]
depth	derinlik	[dærinlik]
volume	hacim	[hadʒim]
area	alan	[alan]

gram	gram	[gram]
milligram	miligram	[miligram]
kilogram	kilogram	[kilogram]
ton	ton	[ton]
pound	libre	[libræ]
ounce	ons	[ons]

meter	metre	[mætræ]
millimeter	milimetre	[milimætræ]
centimeter	santimetre	[santimætræ]
kilometer	kilometre	[kilomætræ]
mile	mil	[miʎ]

inch	inç	[intʃ]
foot	kadem	[kadæm]
yard	yarda	[jarda]

square meter	metre kare	[mætræ karæ]
hectare	hektar	[hæktar]

liter	litre	[litræ]
degree	derece	[dærædʒæ]
volt	volt	[voʎt]
ampere	amper	[ampær]
horsepower	beygir gücü	[bæjgir gydʒy]

quantity	miktar	[miktar]
a little bit of ...	biraz ...	[biraz]
half	yarım	[jarım]

dozen	düzine	[dyzinæ]
piece (item)	adet, tane	[adæt], [tanæ]

size	boyut	[bojut]
scale (map ~)	ölçek	[øʎtʃæk]

minimal (adj)	minimum	[minimum]
the smallest (adj)	en küçük	[æn kytʃuk]
medium (adj)	orta	[orta]
maximal (adj)	maksimum	[maksimum]
the largest (adj)	en büyük	[æn byjuk]

12. Containers

jar (glass)	kavanoz	[kavanoz]
can	teneke	[tænækæ]
bucket	kova	[kova]
barrel	fıçı, varil	[fıtʃı], [varil]

basin (for washing)	leğen	[læ:n]
tank (for liquid, gas)	tank	[taŋk]
hip flask	matara	[matara]
jerrycan	benzin bidonu	[bænzin bidonu]
cistern (tank)	sarnıç	[sarnıtʃ]

mug	kupa	[kupa]
cup (of coffee, etc.)	fincan	[findʒan]
saucer	fincan tabağı	[findʒan tabaı]
glass (tumbler)	bardak	[bardak]
wineglass	kadeh	[kadæ]
saucepan	tencere	[tændʒæræ]

bottle (~ of wine)	şişe	[ʃiʃæ]
neck (of the bottle)	boğaz	[boaz]

carafe	sürahi	[syrahi]
pitcher (earthenware)	testi	[tæsti]
vessel (container)	kap	[kap]
pot (crock)	çömlek	[tʃomlæk]
vase	vazo	[vazo]

bottle (~ of perfume)	şişe	[ʃiʃæ]
vial, small bottle	küçük şişe	[kytʃuk ʃiʃæ]
tube (of toothpaste)	tüp	[typ]

sack (bag)	poşet, torba	[poʃæt], [torba]
bag (paper ~, plastic ~)	çuval	[tʃuval]
pack (of cigarettes, etc.)	paket	[pakæt]

box (e.g., shoebox)	kutu	[kutu]
crate	sandık	[sandık]
basket	sepet	[sæpæt]

MAIN VERBS

13. The most important verbs. Part 1

to advise (vt)	tavsiye etmek	[tavsijæ ætmæk]
to agree (say yes)	razı olmak	[razı olmak]
to answer (vi, vt)	cevap vermek	[dʒævap værmæk]
to apologize (vi)	özür dilemek	[øzyr dilæmæk]
to arrive (vi)	gelmek	[gæʎmæk]
to ask (~ oneself)	sormak	[sormak]
to ask (~ sb to do sth)	rica etmek	[ridʒa ætmæk]
to be (vi)	olmak	[olmak]
to be afraid	korkmak	[korkmak]
to be hungry	yemek istemek	[jæmæk istæmæk]
to be interested in ...	ilgilenmek	[iʎgilænmæk]
to be needed	gerekmek	[gærækmæk]
to be surprised	şaşırmak	[ʃaʃırmak]
to be thirsty	içmek istemek	[itʃmæk istæmæk]
to begin (vt)	başlamak	[baʃlamak]
to belong to ...	... ait olmak	[ait olmak]
to boast (vi)	övünmek	[øvynmæk]
to break (split into pieces)	kırmak	[kırmak]
to call (for help)	çağırmak	[tʃaırmak]
can (v aux)	yapabilmek	[japabiʎmæk]
to catch (vt)	tutmak	[tutmak]
to change (vt)	değiştirmek	[dæiʃtirmæk]
to choose (select)	seçmek	[sætʃmæk]
to come down	aşağı inmek	[aʃaı inmæk]
to come in (enter)	girmek	[girmæk]
to compare (vt)	karşılaştırmak	[karʃılaʃtırmak]
to complain (vi, vt)	şikayet etmek	[ʃikajæt ætmæk]
to confuse (mix up)	ayırt edememek	[ajırt ædæmæmæk]
to continue (vt)	devam etmek	[dævam ætmæk]
to control (vt)	kontrol etmek	[kontroʎ ætmæk]
to cook (dinner)	pişirmek	[piʃirmæk]
to cost (vt)	değerinde olmak	[dæ:rindæ olmak]
to count (add up)	saymak	[sajmak]
to count on ...	... güvenmek	[gyvænmæk]
to create (vt)	oluşturmak	[oluʃturmak]
to cry (weep)	ağlamak	[a:lamak]

14. The most important verbs. Part 2

to deceive (vi, vt)	aldatmak	[aldatmak]
to decorate (tree, street)	süslemek	[syslæmæk]
to defend (a country, etc.)	savunmak	[savunmak]
to demand (request firmly)	talep etmek	[talæp ætmæk]
to dig (vt)	kazmak	[kazmak]
to discuss (vt)	görüşmek	[gøryʃmæk]
to do (vt)	yapmak, etmek	[japmak], [ætmæk]
to doubt (have doubts)	tereddüt etmek	[tæræddyt ætmæk]
to drop (let fall)	düşürmek	[dyʃyrmæk]
to excuse (forgive)	affetmek	[afætmæk]
to exist (vi)	var olmak	[var olmak]
to expect (foresee)	önceden görmek	[øndʒædæn gørmæk]
to explain (vt)	izah etmek	[izah ætmæk]
to fall (vi)	düşmek	[dyʃmæk]
to find (vt)	bulmak	[bulmak]
to finish (vt)	bitirmek	[bitirmæk]
to fly (vi)	uçmak	[utʃmak]
to follow ... (come after)	... takip etmek	[takip ætmæk]
to forget (vi, vt)	unutmak	[unutmak]
to forgive (vt)	affetmek	[afætmæk]
to give (vt)	vermek	[værmæk]
to give a hint	ipucu vermek	[ipudʒu værmæk]
to go (on foot)	yürümek, gitmek	[jurymæk], [gitmæk]
to go for a swim	suya girmek	[suja girmæk]
to go out (from ...)	çıkmak	[tʃıkmak]
to guess right	doğru tahmin etmek	[do:ru tahmin ætmæk]
to have (vt)	sahip olmak	[sahip olmak]
to have breakfast	kahvaltı yapmak	[kahvaltı japmak]
to have dinner	akşam yemeği yemek	[akʃam jæmæi jæmæk]
to have lunch	öğle yemeği yemek	[øjlæ jæmæi jæmæk]
to hear (vt)	duymak	[dujmak]
to help (vt)	yardım etmek	[jardım ætmæk]
to hide (vt)	saklamak	[saklamak]
to hope (vi, vt)	ummak	[ummak]
to hunt (vi, vt)	avlamak	[avlamak]
to hurry (vi)	acele etmek	[adʒælæ ætmæk]

15. The most important verbs. Part 3

to inform (vt)	bilgi vermek	[biʎgi værmæk]
to insist (vi, vt)	ısrar etmek	[ısrar ætmæk]

to insult (vt)	hakaret etmek	[hakaræt ætmæk]
to invite (vt)	davet etmek	[davæt ætmæk]
to joke (vi)	şaka yapmak	[ʃaka japmak]
to keep (vt)	saklamak	[saklamak]
to keep silent	susmak	[susmak]
to kill (vt)	öldürmek	[øldyrmæk]
to know (sb)	tanımak	[tanımak]
to know (sth)	bilmek	[biʎmæk]
to laugh (vi)	gülmek	[gyʎmæk]
to liberate (city, etc.)	özgür bırakmak	[øzgyr bırakmak]
to like (I like ...)	hoşlanmak	[hoʃlanmak]
to look for ... (search)	aramak	[aramak]
to love (sb)	sevmek	[sævmæk]
to make a mistake	hata yapmak	[hata japmak]
to manage, to run	yönetmek	[jonætmæk]
to mean (signify)	anlamına gelmek	[anlamina gæʎmæk]
to mention (talk about)	anmak	[anmak]
to miss (school, etc.)	gelmemek	[gæʎmæmæk]
to notice (see)	farketmek	[farkætmæk]
to object (vi, vt)	itiraz etmek	[itiraz ætmæk]
to observe (see)	gözlemlemek	[gøzlæmlæmæk]
to open (vt)	açmak	[atʃmak]
to order (meal, etc.)	sipariş etmek	[sipariʃ ætmæk]
to order (mil.)	emretmek	[æmrætmæk]
to own (possess)	sahip olmak	[sahip olmak]
to participate (vi)	katılmak	[katılmak]
to pay (vi, vt)	ödemek	[ødæmæk]
to permit (vt)	izin vermek	[izin værmæk]
to plan (vt)	planlamak	[pʎanlamak]
to play (children)	oynamak	[ojnamak]
to pray (vi, vt)	dua etmek	[dua ætmæk]
to prefer (vt)	tercih etmek	[tærdʒih ætmæk]
to promise (vt)	vaat etmek	[va:t ætmæk]
to pronounce (vt)	telâffuz etmek	[tæʎafuz ætmæk]
to propose (vt)	önermek	[ønærmæk]
to punish (vt)	cezalandırmak	[dʒæzalandırmak]
to read (vi, vt)	okumak	[okumak]
to recommend (vt)	tavsiye etmek	[tavsijæ ætmæk]
to refuse (vi, vt)	reddetmek	[ræddætmæk]
to regret (be sorry)	üzülmek	[juzylmæk]
to rent (sth from sb)	kiralamak	[kiralamak]
to repeat (say again)	tekrar etmek	[tækrar ætmæk]
to reserve, to book	rezerve etmek	[ræzærvæ ætmæk]
to run (vi)	koşmak	[koʃmak]

16. The most important verbs. Part 4

to save (rescue)	kurtarmak	[kurtarmak]
to say (~ thank you)	söylemek	[søjlæmæk]
to scold (vt)	sövmek	[søvmæk]
to see (vt)	görmek	[gørmæk]
to sell (vt)	satmak	[satmak]
to send (vt)	göndermek	[gøndærmæk]

to shoot (vi)	ateş etmek	[ataeʃ ætmæk]
to shout (vi)	bağırmak	[baırmak]
to show (vt)	göstermek	[gøstærmæk]
to sign (document)	imzalamak	[imzalamak]
to sit down (vi)	oturmak	[oturmak]
to smile (vi)	gülümsemek	[gylymsæmæk]

to speak (vi, vt)	konuşmak	[konuʃmak]
to steal (money, etc.)	çalmak	[ʧalmak]
to stop (please ~ calling me)	durdurmak	[durdurmak]
to stop (for pause, etc.)	durmak	[durmak]
to study (vt)	öğrenmek	[øjrænmæk]
to swim (vi)	yüzmek	[juzmæk]

to take (vt)	almak	[almak]
to think (vi, vt)	düşünmek	[dyʃynmæk]
to threaten (vt)	tehdit etmek	[tæhdit ætmæk]
to touch (with hands)	ellemek	[ællæmæk]
to translate (vt)	çevirmek	[ʧævirmæk]
to trust (vt)	güvenmek	[gyvænmæk]
to try (attempt)	denemek	[dænæmæk]
to turn (~ to the left)	dönmek	[dønmæk]

to underestimate (vt)	değerini bilmemek	[dæ:rini bilmæmæk]
to understand (vt)	anlamak	[anlamak]
to unite (vt)	birleştirmek	[birlæʃtirmæk]

to wait (vt)	beklemek	[bæklæmæk]
to want (wish, desire)	istemek	[istæmæk]
to warn (vt)	uyarmak	[ujarmak]
to work (vi)	çalışmak	[ʧalıʃmak]
to write (vt)	yazmak	[jazmak]
to write down	not almak	[not almak]

TIME. CALENDAR

17. Weekdays

Monday	**Pazartesi**	[pazartæsi]
Tuesday	**Salı**	[salı]
Wednesday	**Çarşamba**	[tʃarʃamba]
Thursday	**Perşembe**	[pærʃæmbæ]
Friday	**Cuma**	[dʒuma]
Saturday	**Cumartesi**	[dʒumartæsi]
Sunday	**Pazar**	[pazar]
today (adv)	**bugün**	[bugyn]
tomorrow (adv)	**yarın**	[jarın]
the day after tomorrow	**öbür gün**	[øbyr gyn]
yesterday (adv)	**dün**	[dyn]
the day before yesterday	**evvelki gün**	[ævvælki gyn]
day	**gün**	[gyn]
working day	**iş günü**	[iʃ gyny]
public holiday	**bayram günü**	[bajram gyny]
day off	**tatil günü**	[tatil gyny]
weekend	**hafta sonu**	[hafta sonu]
all day long	**bütün gün**	[bytyn gyn]
next day (adv)	**ertesi gün**	[ærtæsi gyn]
two days ago	**iki gün önce**	[iki gyn øndʒæ]
the day before	**bir gün önce**	[bir gyn øndʒæ]
daily (adj)	**günlük**	[gynlyk]
every day (adv)	**her gün**	[hær gyn]
week	**hafta**	[hafta]
last week (adv)	**geçen hafta**	[gætʃæn hafta]
next week (adv)	**gelecek hafta**	[gæʎdʒæk hafta]
weekly (adj)	**haftalık**	[haftalık]
every week (adv)	**her hafta**	[hær hafta]
twice a week	**haftada iki kez**	[haftada iki kæz]
every Tuesday	**her Salı**	[hær salı]

18. Hours. Day and night

morning	**sabah**	[sabah]
in the morning	**sabahleyin**	[sabahlæjın]
noon, midday	**öğle, gün ortası**	[øjlæ], [gyn ortası]

in the afternoon	öğleden sonra	[øjlædæn sonra]
evening	akşam	[akʃam]
in the evening	akşamleyin	[akʃamlæjın]
night	gece	[gædʒæ]
at night	geceleyin	[gædʒælæjın]
midnight	gece yarısı	[gædʒæ jarısı]
second	saniye	[sanijæ]
minute	dakika	[dakika]
hour	saat	[sa:t]
half an hour	yarım saat	[jarım sa:t]
quarter of an hour	çeyrek saat	[tʃæjræk sa:t]
fifteen minutes	on beş dakika	[on bæʃ dakika]
24 hours	yirmi dört saat	[jırmi dørt sa:t]
sunrise	güneşin doğuşu	[gynæʃin douʃu]
dawn	şafak	[ʃafak]
early morning	sabah erken	[sabah ærkæn]
sunset	güneş batışı	[gynæʃ batıʃı]
early in the morning	sabahın köründe	[sabahın køryndæ]
this morning	bu sabah	[bu sabah]
tomorrow morning	yarın sabah	[jarın sabah]
this afternoon	bu ikindi	[bu ikindi]
in the afternoon	öğleden sonra	[øjlædæn sonra]
tomorrow afternoon	yarın öğleden sonra	[jarın øælædæn sonra]
tonight (this evening)	bu akşam	[bu akʃam]
tomorrow night	yarın akşam	[jarın akʃam]
at 3 o'clock sharp	tam saat üçte	[tam sa:t jutʃtæ]
about 4 o'clock	saat dört civarında	[sa:t dørt dʒivarında]
by 12 o'clock	saat on ikiye doğru	[sa:t on ikijæ do:ru]
in 20 minutes	yirmi dakika içinde	[jırmi dakika itʃindæ]
in an hour	bir saat sonra	[bir sa:t sonra]
on time (adv)	zamanında	[zamanında]
a quarter of ...	çeyrek kala	[tʃæjræk kala]
within an hour	bir saat içinde	[bir sa:t itʃindæ]
every 15 minutes	her on beş dakika	[hær on bæʃ dakika]
round the clock	gece gündüz	[gædʒæ gyndyz]

19. Months. Seasons

January	ocak	[odʒak]
February	şubat	[ʃubat]
March	mart	[mart]
April	nisan	[nisan]

May	**mayıs**	[majıs]
June	**haziran**	[haziran]
July	**temmuz**	[tæmmuz]
August	**ağustos**	[a:ustos]
September	**eylül**	[æjlyʎ]
October	**ekim**	[ækim]
November	**kasım**	[kasım]
December	**aralık**	[aralık]
spring	**ilkbahar**	[iʎkbahar]
in spring	**ilkbaharda**	[iʎkbaharda]
spring (as adj)	**ilkbahar**	[iʎkbahar]
summer	**yaz**	[jaz]
in summer	**yazın**	[jazın]
summer (as adj)	**yaz**	[jaz]
fall	**sonbahar**	[sonbahar]
in fall	**sonbaharda**	[sonbaharda]
fall (as adj)	**sonbahar**	[sonbahar]
winter	**kış**	[kıʃ]
in winter	**kışın**	[kıʃin]
winter (as adj)	**kış, kışlık**	[kıʃ], [kıʃlık]
month	**ay**	[aj]
this month	**bu ay**	[bu aj]
next month	**gelecek ay**	[gælædʒæk aj]
last month	**geçen ay**	[gætʃæn aj]
a month ago	**bir ay önce**	[bir aj øndʒæ]
in a month	**bir ay sonra**	[bir aj sonra]
in two months	**iki ay sonra**	[iki aj sonra]
the whole month	**tüm ay**	[tym aj]
all month long	**bütün ay**	[bytyn aj]
monthly (~ magazine)	**aylık**	[ajlık]
monthly (adv)	**her ay**	[hær aj]
every month	**her ay**	[hær aj]
twice a month	**ayda iki kez**	[ajda iki kæz]
year	**yıl, sene**	[jıl], [sænæ]
this year	**bu sene, bu yıl**	[bu sænæ], [bu jıl]
next year	**gelecek sene**	[gælædʒæk sænæ]
last year	**geçen sene**	[gætʃæn sænæ]
a year ago	**bir yıl önce**	[bir jıl øndʒæ]
in a year	**bir yıl sonra**	[bir jıl sonra]
in two years	**iki yıl sonra**	[iki jıl sonra]
the whole year	**tüm yıl**	[tym jıl]
all year long	**bütün yıl**	[bytyn jıl]

every year	her sene	[hær sænæ]
annual (adj)	yıllık	[jıllık]
annually (adv)	her yıl	[hær jıl]
4 times a year	yılda dört kere	[jılda dørt kæræ]

date (e.g., today's ~)	tarih	[tarih]
date (e.g., ~ of birth)	tarih	[tarih]
calendar	takvim	[takvim]

half a year	yarım yıl	[jarım jıl]
six months	altı ay	[altı aj]
season (summer, etc.)	mevsim	[mævsim]
century	yüzyıl	[juz jıl]

TRAVEL. HOTEL

20. Trip. Travel

tourism	**turizm**	[turizm]
tourist	**turist**	[turist]
trip, voyage	**seyahat**	[sæjahat]
adventure	**macera**	[madʒæra]
trip, journey	**gezi**	[gæzi]
vacation	**izin**	[izin]
to be on vacation	**izinli olmak**	[izinli olmak]
rest	**istirahat**	[istirahat]
train	**tren**	[træn]
by train	**trenle**	[trænlæ]
airplane	**uçak**	[utʃak]
by airplane	**uçakla**	[utʃakla]
by car	**arabayla**	[arabajla]
by ship	**gemide**	[gæmidæ]
luggage	**bagaj**	[bagaʒ]
suitcase, luggage	**bavul**	[bavul]
luggage cart	**bagaj arabası**	[bagaʒ arabası]
passport	**pasaport**	[pasaport]
visa	**vize**	[vizæ]
ticket	**bilet**	[bilæt]
air ticket	**uçak bileti**	[utʃak bilæti]
guidebook	**rehber**	[ræhbær]
map	**harita**	[harita]
area (rural ~)	**alan**	[alan]
place, site	**yer**	[jær]
exotic (n)	**egzotik**	[ækzotik]
exotic (adj)	**egzotik**	[ækzotik]
amazing (adj)	**şaşırtıcı**	[ʃaʃırtıdʒı]
group	**grup**	[grup]
excursion	**gezi**	[gæzi]
guide (person)	**rehber**	[ræhbær]

21. Hotel

hotel	otel	[otæʌ]
motel	motel	[motæʌ]
three-star	üç yıldızlı	[jutʃ jıldızlı]
five-star	beş yıldızlı	[bæʃ jıldızlı]
to stay (in hotel, etc.)	kalmak	[kalmak]
room	oda	[oda]
single room	tek kişilik oda	[tæk kiʃilik oda]
double room	iki kişilik oda	[iki kiʃilik oda]
to book a room	oda ayırtmak	[oda aırtmak]
half board	yarım pansiyon	[jarım pansʲon]
full board	tam pansiyon	[tam pansʲon]
with bath	banyolu	[baɲjolu]
with shower	duşlu	[duʃlu]
satellite television	uydu televizyonu	[ujdu tælævizʲonu]
air-conditioner	klima	[klima]
towel	havlu	[havlu]
key	anahtar	[anahtar]
administrator	idareci	[idarædʒi]
chambermaid	hizmetçi	[hizmætʃi]
porter, bellboy	hamal	[hamal]
doorman	kapıcı	[kapıdʒı]
restaurant	restoran	[ræstoran]
pub, bar	bar	[bar]
breakfast	kahvaltı	[kahvaltı]
dinner	akşam yemeği	[akʃam jæmæi]
buffet	açık büfe	[atʃık byfæ]
lobby	lobi	[lobi]
elevator	asansör	[asansør]
DO NOT DISTURB	RAHATSIZ ETMEYIN	[rahatsız ætmæjın]
NO SMOKING	SİGARA İÇİLMEZ	[sigara itʃiʌmæz]

22. Sightseeing

monument	anıt	[anıt]
fortress	kale	[kalæ]
palace	saray	[saraj]
castle	şato	[ʃato]
tower	kule	[kulæ]
mausoleum	anıtkabir	[anıtkabir]

architecture	mimarlık	[mimarlik]
medieval (adj)	ortaçağ	[ortatʃa:]
ancient (adj)	antik, eski	[antik], [æski]
national (adj)	milli	[milli]
well-known (adj)	meşhur	[mæʃhur]

tourist	turist	[turist]
guide (person)	rehber	[ræhbær]
excursion, guided tour	gezi	[gæzi]
to show (vt)	göstermek	[gøstærmæk]
to tell (vt)	anlatmak	[anlatmak]

to find (vt)	bulmak	[bulmak]
to get lost (lose one's way)	kaybolmak	[kajbolmak]
map (e.g., subway ~)	şema	[ʃæma]
map (e.g., city ~)	plan	[pʎan]

souvenir, gift	hediye	[hædijæ]
gift shop	hediyelik eşya mağazası	[hædijælik æʃja ma:zasɪ]
to take pictures	fotoğraf çekmek	[fotoraf tʃækmæk]
to be photographed	fotoğraf çektirmek	[fotoraf tʃæktirmæk]

TRANSPORTATION

23. Airport

airport	havaalanı	[hava:lanı]
airplane	uçak	[utʃak]
airline	hava yolları şirketi	[hava jolları ʃirkæti]
air-traffic controller	hava trafik kontrolörü	[hava trafik kontroløry]

departure	kalkış	[kalkıʃ]
arrival	varış	[varıʃ]
to arrive (by plane)	varmak	[varmak]

departure time	kalkış saati	[kalkıʃ sa:ti]
arrival time	iniş saati	[iniʃ sa:ti]

to be delayed	gecikmek	[gædʒikmæk]
flight delay	gecikme	[gædʒikmæ]

information board	bilgi panosu	[biʎgi panosu]
information	danışma	[danıʃma]
to announce (vt)	anons etmek	[anons ætmæk]
flight (e.g., next ~)	uçuş, sefer	[utʃuʃ], [sæfær]

customs	gümrük	[gymryk]
customs officer	gümrükçü	[gymryktʃu]

customs declaration	gümrük beyannamesi	[gymryk bæjaŋamæsi]
to fill out the declaration	beyanname doldurmak	[bæjaŋamæ doldurmak]
passport control	pasaport kontrol	[pasaport kontroʎ]

luggage	bagaj	[bagaʒ]
hand luggage	el bagajı	[æʎ bagaʒı]
Lost Luggage Desk	kayıp eşya bürosu	[kajıp æʃja byrosu]
luggage cart	bagaj arabası	[bagaʒ arabası]

landing	iniş	[iniʃ]
landing strip	iniş pisti	[iniʃ pisti]
to land (vi)	inmek	[inmæk]
airstairs	uçak merdiveni	[utʃak mærdivæni]

check-in	check-in	[tʃækin]
check-in desk	kontuar check-in	[kontuar tʃækin]
to check-in (vi)	check-in yapmak	[tʃækin japmak]
boarding pass	biniş kartı	[biniʃ kartı]
departure gate	çıkış kapısı	[tʃıkıʃ kapısı]

transit	transit	[transit]
to wait (vi)	beklemek	[bæklæmæk]
departure lounge	bekleme salonu	[bæklæmæ salonu]
to see off	yolcu etmek	[joldʒu ætmæk]
to say goodbye	vedalaşmak	[vædalaʃmak]

24. Airplane

airplane	uçak	[utʃak]
air ticket	uçak bileti	[utʃak bilæti]
airline	hava yolları şirketi	[hava jolları ʃirkæti]
airport	havaalanı	[hava:lanı]
supersonic (adj)	sesüstü	[sæsysty]
captain	kaptan pilot	[kaptan pilot]
crew	ekip	[ækip]
pilot	pilot	[pilot]
flight attendant	hostes	[hostæs]
navigator	seyrüseferci	[sæjrysæfærdʒi]
wings	kanatlar	[kanatlar]
tail	kuyruk	[kujruk]
cockpit	kabin	[kabin]
engine	motor	[motor]
undercarriage	iniş takımı	[iniʃ takımı]
turbine	türbin	[tyrbin]
propeller	pervane	[pærvanæ]
black box	kara kutu	[kara kutu]
control column	kumanda kolu	[kumanda kolu]
fuel	yakıt	[jakıt]
safety card	güvenlik kartı	[gyvænlik kartı]
oxygen mask	oksijen maskesi	[oksiʒæn maskæsi]
uniform	üniforma	[juniforma]
life vest	can yeleği	[dʒan jælæi]
parachute	paraşüt	[paraʃyt]
takeoff	kalkış	[kalkıʃ]
to take off (vi)	kalkmak	[kalkmak]
runway	kalkış pisti	[kalkıʃ pisti]
visibility	görüş	[gøryʃ]
flight (act of flying)	uçuş	[utʃuʃ]
altitude	yükseklik	[juksæklik]
air pocket	hava boşluğu	[hava boʃlu:]
seat	yer	[jær]
headphones	kulaklık	[kulaklık]
folding tray	katlanır tepsi	[katlanır tæpsi]

| airplane window | pencere | [pændʒæræ] |
| aisle | koridor | [koridor] |

25. Train

train	tren	[træn]
suburban train	elektrikli tren	[ælæktrikli træn]
express train	hızlı tren	[hızlı træn]
diesel locomotive	dizel lokomotifi	[dizæʎ lokomotifi]
steam engine	lokomotif	[lokomotif]

| passenger car | vagon | [vagon] |
| dining car | vagon restoran | [vagon ræstoran] |

rails	ray	[raj]
railroad	demir yolu	[dæmir jolu]
railway tie	travers	[traværs]

platform (railway ~)	peron	[pæron]
track (~ 1, 2, etc.)	yol	[jol]
semaphore	semafor	[sæmafor]
station	istasyon	[istasʲon]

engineer	makinist	[makinist]
porter (of luggage)	hamal	[hamal]
train steward	kondüktör	[kondyktør]
passenger	yolcu	[joldʒu]
conductor	kondüktör	[kondyktør]

| corridor (in train) | koridor | [koridor] |
| emergency break | imdat freni | [imdat fræni] |

compartment	kompartıman	[kompartıman]
berth	yatak	[jatak]
upper berth	üst yatak	[just jatak]
lower berth	alt yatak	[alt jatak]
bed linen	yatak takımı	[jatak takımı]

ticket	bilet	[bilæt]
schedule	tarife	[tarifæ]
information display	sefer tarifesi	[sæfær tarifæsi]

to leave, to depart	kalkmak	[kalkmak]
departure (of train)	kalkış	[kalkıʃ]
to arrive (ab. train)	varmak	[varmak]
arrival	varış	[varıʃ]

to arrive by train	trenle gelmek	[trænlæ gæʎmæk]
to get on the train	trene binmek	[trænæ binmæk]
to get off the train	trenden inmek	[trændæn inmæk]

steam engine	lokomotif	[lokomotif]
stoker, fireman	ocakçı	[odʒaktʃı]
firebox	ocak	[odʒak]
coal	kömür	[kømyr]

26. Ship

| ship | gemi | [gæmi] |
| vessel | tekne | [tæknæ] |

steamship	vapur	[vapur]
riverboat	dizel motorlu gemi	[dizæʎ motorlu gæmi]
ocean liner	büyük gemi	[byjuk gæmi]
cruiser	kruvazör	[kruvazør]

yacht	yat	[jat]
tugboat	römorkör	[rømorkør]
barge	yük dubası	[juk dubası]
ferry	feribot	[færibot]

| sailing ship | yelkenli gemi | [jælkænli gæmi] |
| brigantine | gulet | [gulæt] |

| ice breaker | buzkıran | [buzkıran] |
| submarine | denizaltı | [dænizaltı] |

boat (flat-bottomed ~)	kayık	[kajık]
dinghy	filika	[filika]
lifeboat	cankurtaran filikası	[dʒaŋkurtaran filikası]
motorboat	sürat teknesi	[syrat tæknæsi]

captain	kaptan	[kaptan]
seaman	tayfa	[tajfa]
sailor	denizci	[dænizdʒi]
crew	mürettebat	[myrættæbat]

boatswain	lostromo	[lostromo]
ship's boy	miço	[mitʃo]
cook	gemi aşçısı	[gæmi aʃtʃısı]
ship's doctor	gemi doktoru	[gæmi doktoru]

deck	güverte	[gyværtæ]
mast	direk	[diræk]
sail	yelken	[jæʎkæn]

hold	ambar	[ambar]
bow (prow)	geminin baş tarafı	[gæminin baʃ tarafı]
stern	kıç	[kıtʃ]
oar	kürek	[kyræk]
screw propeller	pervane	[pærvanæ]

cabin	kamara	[kamara]
wardroom	subay yemek salonu	[subaj jæmæk salonu]
engine room	makine dairesi	[makinæ dairæsi]
bridge	kaptan köprüsü	[kaptan køprysy]
radio room	telsiz odası	[tælsiz odası]
wave (radio)	dalga	[dalga]
logbook	gemi jurnali	[gæmi ʒurnalı]
spyglass	tek dürbün	[tæk dyrbyn]
bell	çan	[tʃan]
flag	bayrak	[bajrak]
rope (mooring ~)	halat	[halat]
knot (bowline, etc.)	düğüm	[dyjum]
deckrail	vardavela	[vardavæla]
gangway	iskele	[iskælæ]
anchor	çapa, demir	[tʃapa], [dæmir]
to weigh anchor	demir almak	[dæmir almak]
to drop anchor	demir atmak	[dæmir atmak]
anchor chain	çapa zinciri	[tʃapa zindʒiri]
port (harbor)	liman	[liman]
berth, wharf	iskele, rıhtım	[iskælæ], [rihtim]
to berth (moor)	yanaşmak	[janaʃmak]
to cast off	iskeleden ayrılmak	[iskælædæn ajrılmak]
trip, voyage	seyahat	[sæjahat]
cruise (sea trip)	gemi turu	[gæmi turu]
course (route)	seyir	[sæjır]
route (itinerary)	rota	[rota]
fairway	seyir koridoru	[sæjır koridoru]
shallows (shoal)	sığlık	[sıːlık]
to run aground	karaya oturmak	[karaja oturmak]
storm	fırtına	[fırtına]
signal	sinyal	[sinjaʎ]
to sink (vi)	batmak	[batmak]
SOS	SOS	[æs o æs]
ring buoy	can simidi	[dʒan simidi]

CITY

27. Urban transportation

bus	otobüs	[otobys]
streetcar	tramvay	[tramvaj]
trolley	troleybüs	[trolæjbys]
route (of bus)	rota	[rota]
number (e.g., bus ~)	numara	[numara]
to go by ...	... gitmek	[gitmæk]
to get on (~ the bus)	... binmek	[binmæk]
to get off ...	... inmek	[inmæk]
stop (e.g., bus ~)	durak	[durak]
next stop	sonraki durak	[sonraki durak]
terminus	son durak	[son durak]
schedule	tarife	[tarifæ]
to wait (vt)	beklemek	[bæklæmæk]
ticket	bilet	[bilæt]
fare	bilet fiyatı	[bilæt fijatı]
cashier (ticket seller)	kasiyer	[kasijær]
ticket inspection	bilet kontrolü	[bilæt kontroly]
conductor	kondüktör	[kondyktør]
to be late (for ...)	gecikmek	[gædʒikmæk]
to miss (~ the train, etc.)	... kaçırmak	[katʃırmak]
to be in a hurry	acele etmek	[adʒælæ ætmæk]
taxi, cab	taksi	[taksi]
taxi driver	taksici	[taksidʒi]
by taxi	taksiyle	[taksi:læ]
taxi stand	taksi durağı	[taksi duraı]
to call a taxi	taksi çağırmak	[taksi tʃaırmak]
to take a taxi	taksi tutmak	[taksi tutmak]
traffic	trafik	[trafik]
traffic jam	trafik sıkışıklığı	[trafik sıkıʃıklı:]
rush hour	bitirim ikili	[bitirim ikili]
to park (vi)	park etmek	[park ætmæk]
to park (vt)	park etmek	[park ætmæk]
parking lot	park yeri	[park jæri]
subway	metro	[mætro]
station	istasyon	[istasʲon]

to take the subway	metroya binmek	[mætroja binmæk]
train	tren	[træn]
train station	istasyon	[istasʲon]

28. City. Life in the city

city, town	kent, şehir	[kænt], [ʃæhir]
capital city	başkent	[baʃkænt]
village	köy	[køj]

city map	şehir planı	[ʃæhir planı]
downtown	şehir merkezi	[ʃæhir mærkæzi]
suburb	varoş	[varoʃ]
suburban (adj)	banliyö	[banʎjo]

outskirts	şehir kenarı	[ʃæhir kænarı]
environs (suburbs)	çevre	[tʃævræ]
city block	mahalle	[mahalæ]
residential block	yerleşim bölgesi	[jærlæʃim bøʎgæsi]

traffic	trafik	[trafik]
traffic lights	trafik ışıkları	[trafik iʃıkları]
public transportation	toplu taşıma	[toplu taʃima]
intersection	kavşak	[kavʃak]

crosswalk	yaya geçidi	[jaja gætʃidi]
pedestrian underpass	yeraltı geçidi	[jæraltı gætʃidi]
to cross (vt)	geçmek	[gætʃmæk]
pedestrian	yaya	[jaja]
sidewalk	yaya kaldırımı	[jaja kaldırımı]

bridge	köprü	[køpry]
bank (riverbank)	rıhtım	[rıhtım]

allée	park yolu	[park jolu]
park	park	[park]
boulevard	bulvar	[buʎvar]
square	meydan	[mæjdan]
avenue (wide street)	geniş cadde	[gæniʃ dʒaddæ]
street	sokak, cadde	[sokak], [dʒaddæ]
side street	ara sokak	[ara sokak]
dead end	çıkmaz sokak	[tʃıkmaz sokak]

house	ev	[æv]
building	bina	[bina]
skyscraper	gökdelen	[gøkdælæn]

facade	cephe	[dʒæphæ]
roof	çatı	[tʃatı]
window	pencere	[pændʒæræ]

arch	kemer	[kæmær]
column	sütün	[sytyn]
corner	köşe	[køʃæ]

store window	vitrin	[vitrin]
store sign	levha	[lævha]
poster	afiş	[afiʃ]
advertising poster	reklam panosu	[ræklam panosu]
billboard	reklam panosu	[ræklam panosu]

garbage, trash	çöp	[tʃop]
garbage can	çöp tenekesi	[tʃop tænækæsi]
to litter (vi)	çöp atmak	[tʃop atmak]
garbage dump	çöplük	[tʃoplyk]

phone booth	telefon kulübesi	[tælæfon kylybæsi]
lamppost	fener direği	[fænær diræi]
bench (park ~)	bank	[baŋk]

police officer	erkek polis	[ærkæk polis]
police	polis	[polis]
beggar	dilenci	[dilændʒi]
homeless, bum	evsiz	[ævsiz]

29. Urban institutions

store	mağaza	[ma:za]
drugstore, pharmacy	eczane	[ædʒzanæ]
optical store	optik	[optik]
shopping mall	alışveriş merkezi	[alıʃværiʃ mærkæzi]
supermarket	süpermarket	[sypærmarkæt]

bakery	ekmekçi dükkânı	[ækmæktʃi dykkanı]
baker	fırıncı	[fırındʒı]
candy store	pastane	[pastanæ]
grocery store	bakkaliye	[bakkalijæ]
butcher shop	kasap dükkânı	[kasap dykkanı]

| produce store | manav | [manav] |
| market | çarşı | [tʃarʃı] |

coffee house	kahvehane	[kahvæhanæ]
restaurant	restoran	[ræstoran]
pub	birahane	[birahanæ]
pizzeria	pizzacı	[pizadʒı]

hair salon	kuaför salonu	[kuafør salonu]
post office	postane	[postanæ]
dry cleaners	kuru temizleme	[kuru tæmizlæmæ]
photo studio	fotoğraf stüdyosu	[fotoraf stydʲosu]

shoe store	ayakkabı mağazası	[ajakkabı ma:zası]
bookstore	kitabevi	[kitabævi]
sporting goods store	spor mağazası	[spor ma:zası]
clothes repair	elbise tamiri	[æʎbisæ tamiri]
formal wear rental	giysi kiralama	[gijsı kiralama]
movie rental store	film kiralama	[film kiralama]
circus	sirk	[sirk]
zoo	hayvanat bahçesi	[hajvanat bahtʃæsi]
movie theater	sinema	[sinæma]
museum	müze	[myzæ]
library	kütüphane	[kytyphanæ]
theater	tiyatro	[tijatro]
opera	opera	[opæra]
nightclub	gece kulübü	[gædʒæ kulyby]
casino	kazino	[kazino]
mosque	cami	[dʒami]
synagogue	sinagog	[sinagog]
cathedral	katedral	[katædral]
temple	ibadethane	[ibadæthanæ]
church	kilise	[kilisæ]
college	enstitü	[ænstity]
university	üniversite	[juniværesitæ]
school	okul	[okul]
prefecture	belediye	[bælædijæ]
city hall	belediye	[bælædijæ]
hotel	otel	[otæʎ]
bank	banka	[baŋka]
embassy	elçilik	[æʎtʃilik]
travel agency	seyahat acentesi	[sæjahat adʒæntæsi]
information office	danışma bürosu	[danıʃma byrosu]
money exchange	döviz bürosu	[døviz byrosu]
subway	metro	[mætro]
hospital	hastane	[hastanæ]
gas station	benzin istasyonu	[bænzin istasʲonu]
parking lot	park yeri	[park jæri]

30. Signs

store sign	levha	[lævha]
notice (written text)	yazı	[jazı]
poster	poster, afiş	[postær], [afiʃ]

direction sign	işaret	[iʃaræt]
arrow (sign)	ok	[ok]
caution	ikaz, uyarı	[ikaz], [ujarı]
warning sign	uyarı	[ujarı]
to warn (vt)	uyarmak	[ujarmak]
day off	tatil günü	[tatil gyny]
timetable (schedule)	tarife	[tarifæ]
opening hours	çalışma saatleri	[tʃalıʃma sa:tlæri]
WELCOME!	HOŞ GELDİNİZ	[hoʃ gældiniz]
ENTRANCE	GİRİŞ	[giriʃ]
EXIT	ÇIKIŞ	[tʃıkıʃ]
PUSH	İTİNİZ	[itiniz]
PULL	ÇEKİNİZ	[tʃækiniz]
OPEN	AÇIK	[atʃık]
CLOSED	KAPALI	[kapalı]
WOMEN	BAYAN	[bajan]
MEN	BAY	[baj]
DISCOUNTS	İNDİRİM	[indirim]
SALE	UCUZLUK	[udʒuzluk]
NEW!	YENİ	[jæni]
FREE	BEDAVA	[bædava]
ATTENTION!	DİKKAT!	[dikkat]
NO VACANCIES	BOS YER YOK	[bos jær jok]
RESERVED	REZERVE	[ræzærvæ]
ADMINISTRATION	MÜDÜR	[mydyr]
STAFF ONLY	PERSONEL HARİCİ GİREMEZ	[pærsonæl haridʒi giræmæz]
BEWARE OF THE DOG!	DİKKAT KÖPEK VAR	[dikkat køpæk var]
NO SMOKING	SİGARA İÇİLMEZ	[sigara itʃiʎmæz]
DO NOT TOUCH!	DOKUNMAK YASAKTIR	[dokunmak jasaktır]
DANGEROUS	TEHLİKELİ	[tæhlikæli]
DANGER	TEHLİKE	[tæhlikæ]
HIGH TENSION	YÜKSEK GERİLİM	[juksæk gærilim]
NO SWIMMING!	SUYA GİRMEK YASAKTIR	[suja girmæk jasaktır]
OUT OF ORDER	HİZMET DIŞI	[hizmæt diʃı]
FLAMMABLE	YANICI MADDE	[janidʒi maddæ]
FORBIDDEN	YASAKTIR	[jasaktır]
NO TRESPASSING!	GİRMEK YASAKTIR	[girmæk jasaktır]
WET PAINT	DİKKAT ISLAK BOYA	[dikkat ıslak boja]

31. Shopping

to buy (purchase)	satın almak	[satın almak]
purchase	satın alınan şey	[satın alınan ʃæj]
to go shopping	alışverişe gitmek	[alıʃværiʃæ gitmæk]
shopping	alışveriş	[alıʃværiʃ]
to be open (ab. store)	çalışmak	[ʧalıʃmak]
to be closed	kapanmak	[kapanmak]
footwear	ayakkabı	[ajakkabı]
clothes, clothing	elbise	[æʌbisæ]
cosmetics	kozmetik	[kozmætik]
food products	gıda ürünleri	[gıda jurynlæri]
gift, present	hediye	[hædijæ]
salesman	satıcı	[satıʤı]
saleswoman	satıcı kadın	[satıʤı kadın]
check out, cash desk	kasa	[kasa]
mirror	ayna	[ajna]
counter (in shop)	tezgâh	[tæzgʲah]
fitting room	deneme kabini	[dænæmæ kabini]
to try on	prova yapmak	[prova japmak]
to fit (ab. dress, etc.)	uymak	[ujmak]
to like (I like ...)	hoşlanmak	[hoʃlanmak]
price	fiyat	[fijat]
price tag	fiyat etiketi	[fijat ætikætlæri]
to cost (vt)	değerinde olmak	[dæ:rindæ olmak]
How much?	Kaç?	[katʃ]
discount	indirim	[indirim]
inexpensive (adj)	masrafsız	[masrafsıs]
cheap (adj)	ucuz	[uʤuz]
expensive (adj)	pahalı	[pahalı]
It's expensive	bu pahalıdır	[bu pahalıdır]
rental (n)	kira	[kira]
to rent (~ a tuxedo)	kiralamak	[kiralamak]
credit	kredi	[krædi]
on credit (adv)	krediyle	[krædijlæ]

CLOTHING & ACCESSORIES

32. Outerwear. Coats

clothes	elbise, kıyafet	[æʎbisæ], [kıjafæt]
outer clothes	üst kıyafet	[just kıjafæt]
winter clothes	kışlık kıyafet	[kıʃlık kıjafæt]

overcoat	palto	[paʎto]
fur coat	kürk manto	[kyrk manto]
fur jacket	kürk ceket	[kyrk dʒækæt]
down coat	ceket aşağı	[dʒækæt aʃaı]

jacket (e.g., leather ~)	ceket	[dʒækæt]
raincoat	trençkot	[træntʃkot]
waterproof (adj)	su geçirmez	[su gætʃirmæz]

33. Men's & women's clothing

shirt	gömlek	[gømlæk]
pants	pantolon	[pantolon]
jeans	kot pantolon	[kot pantolon]
jacket (of man's suit)	ceket	[dʒækæt]
suit	takım elbise	[takım æʎbisæ]

dress (frock)	elbise, kıyafet	[æʎbisæ], [kıjafæt]
skirt	etek	[ætæk]
blouse	gömlek, bluz	[gømlæk], [bluz]
knitted jacket	hırka	[hırka]
jacket (of woman's suit)	ceket	[dʒækæt]

T-shirt	tişört	[tiʃort]
shorts (short trousers)	şort	[ʃort]
tracksuit	eşofman	[æʃofman]
bathrobe	bornoz	[bornoz]
pajamas	pijama	[piʒama]

| sweater | süveter | [syvætær] |
| pullover | pulover | [pulovær] |

vest	yelek	[jælæk]
tailcoat	frak	[frak]
tuxedo	smokin	[smokin]
uniform	üniforma	[juniforma]

workwear	iş elbisesi	[iʃ æʌbisæsi]
overalls	tulum	[tulum]
coat (e.g., doctor's smock)	önlük	[ønlyk]

34. Clothing. Underwear

underwear	iç çamaşırı	[itʃ tʃamaʃırı]
undershirt (A-shirt)	atlet	[atlæt]
socks	kısa çorap	[kısa tʃorap]

nightgown	gecelik	[gædʒælik]
bra	sutyen	[sutˈæn]
knee highs	diz hizası çorap	[diz hizası tʃorap]
tights	külotlu çorap	[kyløtly tʃorap]
stockings (thigh highs)	çorap	[tʃorap]
bathing suit	mayo	[majo]

35. Headwear

hat	şapka	[ʃapka]
fedora	fötr şapka	[føtr ʃapka]
baseball cap	beyzbol şapkası	[bæjzbol ʃapkası]
flatcap	kasket	[kaskæt]

beret	bere	[bæræ]
hood	kapüşon	[kapyʃon]
panama hat	panama	[panama]
knitted hat	örgü şapka	[ørgy ʃapka]

| headscarf | başörtüsü | [baʃ ørtysy] |
| women's hat | kadın şapkası | [kadın ʃapkası] |

hard hat	baret, kask	[baræt], [kask]
garrison cap	kayık kep	[kajık kæp]
helmet	kask	[kask]

| derby | melon şapka | [mælon ʃapka] |
| top hat | silindir şapka | [silindir ʃapka] |

36. Footwear

footwear	ayakkabı	[ajakkabı]
ankle boots	potinler	[potinlær]
shoes (low-heeled ~)	ayakkabılar	[ajakkabılar]
boots (cowboy ~)	çizmeler	[tʃizmælær]
slippers	terlik	[tærlik]

tennis shoes	**tenis ayakkabısı**	[tænis ajakkabısı]
sneakers	**spor ayakkabısı**	[spor ajakkabısı]
sandals	**sandalet**	[sandalæt]
cobbler	**ayakkabıcı**	[ajakkabıdʒı]
heel	**topuk**	[topuk]
pair (of shoes)	**bir çift ayakkabı**	[birʲ tʃift ajakkabı]
shoestring	**bağ**	[ba:]
to lace (vt)	**bağlamak**	[ba:lamak]
shoehorn	**kaşık**	[kaʃık]
shoe polish	**ayakkabı boyası**	[ajakkabı bojası]

37. Personal accessories

gloves	**eldiven**	[æʎdivæn]
mittens	**tek parmaklı eldiven**	[tæk parmaklı æʎdivæn]
scarf (muffler)	**atkı**	[atkı]
glasses	**gözlük**	[gøzlyk]
frame (eyeglass ~)	**çerçeve**	[tʃærtʃævæ]
umbrella	**şemsiye**	[ʃæmsijæ]
walking stick	**baston**	[baston]
hairbrush	**saç fırçası**	[satʃ firtʃası]
fan	**yelpaze**	[jælpazæ]
necktie	**kravat**	[kravat]
bow tie	**papyon**	[papʲon]
suspenders	**pantolon askısı**	[pantolon askısı]
handkerchief	**mendil**	[mændiʎ]
comb	**tarak**	[tarak]
barrette	**toka**	[toka]
hairpin	**firkete**	[firkætæ]
buckle	**kemer tokası**	[kæmær tokası]
belt	**kemer**	[kæmær]
shoulder strap	**kayış**	[kajıʃ]
bag (handbag)	**çanta**	[tʃanta]
purse	**bayan çantası**	[bajan tʃantası]
backpack	**arka çantası**	[arka tʃantası]

38. Clothing. Miscellaneous

fashion	**moda**	[moda]
in vogue (adj)	**modaya uygun**	[modaja ujgun]
fashion designer	**modelci**	[modæʎdʒi]

collar	yaka	[jaka]
pocket	cep	[dʒæp]
pocket (as adj)	cep	[dʒæp]
sleeve	kol	[kol]
hanging loop	askı	[askı]
fly (on trousers)	pantolon fermuarı	[pantolon færmuarı]

zipper (fastener)	fermuar	[færmuar]
fastener	kopça	[koptʃa]
button	düğme	[dyjmæ]
buttonhole	düğme iliği	[dyjmæ ili:]
to come off (ab. button)	kopmak	[kopmak]

to sew (vi, vt)	dikmek	[dikmæk]
to embroider (vi, vt)	nakış işlemek	[nakıʃ iʃlæmæk]
embroidery	nakış	[nakıʃ]
sewing needle	iğne	[i:næ]
thread	iplik	[iplik]
seam	dikiş	[dikiʃ]

to get dirty (vi)	kirlenmek	[kirlænmæk]
stain (mark, spot)	leke	[lækæ]
to crease, crumple (vi)	buruşmak	[buruʃmak]
to tear (vt)	yırtmak	[jırtmak]
clothes moth	güve	[gyvæ]

39. Personal care. Cosmetics

toothpaste	diş macunu	[diʃ madʒunu]
toothbrush	diş fırçası	[diʃ fırtʃası]
to brush one's teeth	dişlerini fırçalamak	[diʃlærini fırtʃalamak]

razor	jilet	[ʒilæt]
shaving cream	tıraş kremi	[tıraʃ kræmi]
to shave (vi)	tıraş olmak	[tıraʃ olmak]

| soap | sabun | [sabun] |
| shampoo | şampuan | [ʃampuan] |

scissors	makas	[makas]
nail file	tırnak törpüsü	[tırnak tørpysy]
nail clippers	tırnak makası	[tırnak makası]
tweezers	cımbız	[dʒımbız]

cosmetics	kozmetik	[kozmætik]
face mask	yüz maskesi	[juz maskæsi]
manicure	manikür	[manikyr]
to have a manicure	manikür yapmak	[manikyr japmak]
pedicure	pedikür	[pædikyr]
make-up bag	makyaj çantası	[makjaʒ tʃantası]

face powder	pudra	[pudra]
powder compact	pudralık	[pudralık]
blusher	allık	[allık]
perfume (bottled)	parfüm	[parfym]
toilet water (perfume)	parfüm suyu	[parfym suju]
lotion	losyon	[losʲon]
cologne	kolonya	[koloɲja]
eyeshadow	far	[far]
eyeliner	göz kalemi	[gøz kalæmi]
mascara	rimel	[rimæʎ]
lipstick	ruj	[ruʒ]
nail polish, enamel	oje	[oʒæ]
hair spray	saç spreyi	[satʃ spræjı]
deodorant	deodorant	[dæodorant]
cream	krem	[kræm]
face cream	yüz kremi	[juz kræmi]
hand cream	el kremi	[æʎ kræmi]
anti-wrinkle cream	kırışıklık giderici krem	[kırıʃıklık gidæridʒi kræm]
day (as adj)	günlük	[gynlyk]
night (as adj)	gece	[gædʒæ]
tampon	tampon	[tampon]
toilet paper	tuvalet kağıdı	[tuvalæt kaıdı]
hair dryer	saç kurutma makinesi	[satʃ kurutma makinæsi]

40. Watches. Clocks

watch (wristwatch)	el saati	[æʎ sa:ti]
dial	kadran	[kadran]
hand (of clock, watch)	akrep, yelkovan	[akræp], [jælkovan]
metal watch band	metal kordon	[metaʎ kordon]
watch strap	kayış	[kajıʃ]
battery	pil	[piʎ]
to be dead (battery)	bitmek	[bitmæk]
to change a battery	pil değiştirmek	[piʎ dæiʃtirmæk]
to run fast	ileri gitmek	[ilæri gitmæk]
to run slow	geride kalmak	[gæridæ kalmak]
wall clock	duvar saati	[duvar sa:ti]
hourglass	kum saati	[kum sa:ti]
sundial	güneş saati	[gynæʃ sa:ti]
alarm clock	çalar saat	[tʃalar sa:t]
watchmaker	saatçi	[sa:tʃi]
to repair (vt)	tamir etmek	[tamir ætmæk]

EVERYDAY EXPERIENCE

41. Money

money	para	[para]
currency exchange	kambiyo	[kambijo]
exchange rate	kur	[kur]
ATM	bankamatik	[baŋkamatik]
coin	para	[para]
dollar	dolar	[dolar]
euro	Euro	[juro]
lira	liret	[liræt]
Deutschmark	Alman markı	[alman markı]
franc	frank	[fraŋk]
pound sterling	İngiliz sterlini	[iŋiliz stærlini]
yen	yen	[jæn]
debt	borç	[bortʃ]
debtor	borçlu	[bortʃlu]
to lend (money)	borç vermek	[bortʃ værmæk]
to borrow (vi, vt)	borç almak	[bortʃ almak]
bank	banka	[baŋka]
account	hesap	[hæsap]
to deposit into the account	para yatırmak	[para jatırmak]
to withdraw (vt)	hesaptan çekmek	[hæsaptan tʃækmæk]
credit card	kredi kartı	[krædi kartı]
cash	nakit para	[nakit para]
check	çek	[tʃæk]
to write a check	çek yazmak	[tʃæk jazmak]
checkbook	çek defteri	[tʃæk dæftæri]
wallet	cüzdan	[dʒyzdan]
change purse	para cüzdanı	[para dʒyzdanı]
billfold	cüzdan	[dʒyzdan]
safe	para kasası	[para kasası]
heir	mirasçı	[mirastʃı]
inheritance	miras	[miras]
fortune (wealth)	varlık	[varlık]
lease, rent	kira	[kira]
rent money	ev kirası	[æv kirası]

to rent (sth from sb)	kiralamak	[kiralamak]
price	fiyat	[fijat]
cost	maliyet	[malijæt]
sum	toplam	[toplam]

to spend (vt)	harcamak	[hardʒamak]
expenses	masraflar	[masraflar]
to economize (vi, vt)	idareli kullanmak	[idaræli kullanmak]
economical	tutumlu	[tutumlu]

to pay (vi, vt)	ödemek	[ødæmæk]
payment	ödeme	[ødæmæ]
change (give the ~)	para üstü	[para justy]

tax	vergi	[værgi]
fine	ceza	[dʒæza]
to fine (vt)	ceza kesmek	[dʒæza kæsmæk]

42. Post. Postal service

post office	postane	[postanæ]
mail (letters, etc.)	posta	[posta]
mailman	postacı	[postadʒɪ]
opening hours	çalışma saatleri	[tʃalɪʃma sa:tlæri]

letter	mektup	[mæktup]
registered letter	taahhütlü mektup	[ta:hytly mæktup]
postcard	kart	[kart]
telegram	telgraf	[tælgraf]
parcel	koli	[koli]
money transfer	para havalesi	[para havalæsi]

to receive (vt)	almak	[almak]
to send (vt)	göndermek	[gøndærmæk]
sending	gönderme	[gøndærmæ]

address	adres	[adræs]
ZIP code	endeks, indeks	[ændæks], [indæks]
sender	gönderen	[gøndæræn]
receiver, addressee	alıcı	[alɪdʒɪ]

| name | ad, isim | [ad], [isim] |
| family name | soyadı | [sojadɪ] |

rate (of postage)	tarife	[tarifæ]
standard (adj)	normal	[normaʎ]
economical (adj)	ekonomik	[ækonomik]

| weight | ağırlık | [aɪrlɪk] |
| to weigh up (vt) | tartmak | [tartmak] |

envelope	zarf	[zarf]
postage stamp	pul	[pul]

43. Banking

bank	banka	[baŋka]
branch (of bank, etc.)	banka şubesi	[baŋka ʃubæsı]

bank clerk, consultant	danışman	[danıʃman]
manager (director)	yönetici	[jonætidʒi]

banking account	hesap	[hæsap]
account number	hesap numarası	[hæsap numarası]

checking account	çek hesabı	[tʃæk hæsabı]
savings account	mevduat hesabı	[mævduat hæsabı]

to open an account	hesap açmak	[hæsap atʃmak]
to close the account	hesap kapatmak	[hæsap kapatmak]

to deposit into the account	para yatırmak	[para jatırmak]
to withdraw (vt)	hesaptan çekmek	[hæsaptan tʃækmæk]

deposit	mevduat	[mævduat]
to make a deposit	depozito vermek	[dæpozito værmæk]

wire transfer	havale	[havalæ]
to wire, to transfer	havale etmek	[havalæ ætmæk]

sum	toplam	[toplam]
How much?	Kaç?	[katʃ]

signature	imza	[imza]
to sign (vt)	imzalamak	[imzalamak]

credit card	kredi kartı	[krædi kartı]
code	kod	[kod]

credit card number	kredi kartı numarası	[krædi kartı numarası]
ATM	bankamatik	[baŋkamatik]

check	çek	[tʃæk]
to write a check	çek yazmak	[tʃæk jazmak]
checkbook	çek defteri	[tʃæk dæftæri]

loan (bank ~)	kredi	[krædi]
to apply for a loan	krediye başvurmak	[krædijæ baʃvurmak]
to get a loan	kredi almak	[krædi almak]
to give a loan	kredi vermek	[krædi værmæk]
guarantee	garanti	[garanti]

44. Telephone. Phone conversation

telephone	telefon	[tælæfon]
mobile phone	cep telefonu	[dʒæp tælæfonu]
answering machine	telesekreter	[tælæsækrætær]
to call (telephone)	telefonla aramak	[tælæfonla aramak]
phone call	arama, görüşme	[arama], [gøryʃmæ]
to dial a number	numarayı aramak	[numarajı aramak]
Hello!	Alo!	[alø]
to ask (vt)	sormak	[sormak]
to answer (vi, vt)	cevap vermek	[dʒævap værmæk]
to hear (vt)	duymak	[dujmak]
well (adv)	iyi	[ijı]
not well (adv)	kötü	[køty]
noises (interference)	parazit	[parazit]
receiver	telefon ahizesi	[tælæfon ahizæsi]
to pick up (~ the phone)	açmak telefonu	[atʃmak tælæfonu]
to hang up (~ the phone)	telefonu kapatmak	[tælæfonu kapatmak]
busy (adj)	meşgul	[mæʃguʎ]
to ring (ab. phone)	çalmak	[tʃalmak]
telephone book	telefon rehberi	[tælæfon ræhbæri]
local (adj)	şehiriçi	[ʃæhiritʃi]
local call	şehiriçi görüşme	[ʃæhiritʃi gøryʃmæ]
long distance (~ call)	şehirlerarası	[ʃæhirlerarası]
long-distance call	şehirlerarası görüşme	[ʃæhirlerarası gøryʃmæ]
international (adj)	uluslararası	[uluslar arası]
international call	uluslararası görüşme	[uluslararası gøryʃmæ]

45. Mobile telephone

mobile phone	cep telefonu	[dʒæp tælæfonu]
display	ekran	[ækran]
button	düğme	[dyjmæ]
SIM card	SIM kartı	[simkartı]
battery	pil	[piʎ]
to be dead (battery)	bitmek	[bitmæk]
charger	şarj cihazı	[ʃarʒ dʒihazı]
menu	menü	[mæny]
settings	ayarlar	[ajarlar]
tune (melody)	melodi	[mælodi]
to select (vt)	seçmek	[sætʃmæk]

T&P Books. Turkish vocabulary for English speakers - 3000 words

calculator	hesaplamalar	[hæsaplamanar]
voice mail	telesekreter	[tælæsækrætær]
alarm clock	çalar saat	[tʃalar saːt]
contacts	rehber	[ræhbær]
SMS (text message)	SMS mesajı	[æsæmæs mæsaʒi]
subscriber	abone	[abonæ]

46. Stationery

ballpoint pen	tükenmez kalem	[tykænmæz kalæm]
fountain pen	dolma kalem	[dolma kalæm]

pencil	kurşun kalem	[kurʃun kalæm]
highlighter	fosforlu kalem	[fosforlu kalæm]
felt-tip pen	keçeli kalem	[kætʃæli kalæm]

notepad	not defteri	[not dæftæri]
agenda (diary)	ajanda	[aʒanda]

ruler	cetvel	[dʒætvæʎ]
calculator	hesap makinesi	[hæsap makinæsi]
eraser	silgi	[siʎgi]
thumbtack	raptiye	[raptijæ]
paper clip	ataş	[ataʃ]

glue	yapıştırıcı	[japıʃtırıdʒı]
stapler	zımba	[zımba]
hole punch	delgeç	[dæʎgætʃ]
pencil sharpener	kalemtıraş	[kalæm tıraʃ]

47. Foreign languages

language	dil	[diʎ]
foreign language	yabancı dil	[jabandʒı diʎ]
to study (vt)	öğrenim görmek	[øjrænim gørmæk]
to learn (language, etc.)	öğrenmek	[øjrænmæk]

to read (vi, vt)	okumak	[okumak]
to speak (vi, vt)	konuşmak	[konuʃmak]
to understand (vt)	anlamak	[anlamak]
to write (vt)	yazmak	[jazmak]

fast (adv)	çabuk	[tʃabuk]
slowly (adv)	yavaş	[javaʃ]
fluently (adv)	akıcı bir şekilde	[akıdʒı bir ʃækiʎdæ]
rules	kurallar	[kurallar]
grammar	gramer	[gramær]

56

vocabulary	kelime hazinesi	[kælimæ hazinæsi]
phonetics	fonetik	[fonætik]
textbook	ders kitabı	[dærs kitabı]
dictionary	sözlük	[søzlyk]
teach-yourself book	öz eğitim rehberi	[øz æitim ræhbæri]
phrasebook	konuşma kılavuzu	[konuʃma kılavuzu]
cassette	kaset	[kasæt]
videotape	videokaset	[vidæokasæt]
CD, compact disc	CD	[sidi]
DVD	DVD	[dividi]
alphabet	alfabe	[aʎfabæ]
to spell (vt)	hecelemek	[hædʒælæmæk]
pronunciation	telaffuz	[tælaffyz]
accent	aksan	[aksan]
with an accent	aksan ile	[aksan ilæ]
without an accent	aksansız	[aksansız]
word	kelime	[kælimæ]
meaning	mana	[mana]
course (e.g., a French ~)	kurslar	[kurslar]
to sign up	yazılmak	[jazılmak]
teacher	öğretmen	[øjrætmæn]
translation (process)	çeviri	[tʃæviri]
translation (text, etc.)	tercüme	[tærdʒymæ]
translator	çevirmen	[tʃævirmæn]
interpreter	tercüman	[tærdʒyman]
polyglot	birçok dil bilen	[birtʃok diʎ bilæn]
memory	hafıza	[hafıza]

MEALS. RESTAURANT

48. Table setting

spoon	kaşık	[kaʃık]
knife	bıçak	[bıtʃak]
fork	çatal	[tʃatal]
cup (of coffee)	fincan	[findʒan]
plate (dinner ~)	tabak	[tabak]
saucer	fincan tabağı	[findʒan tabaı]
napkin (on table)	peçete	[pætʃætæ]
toothpick	kürdan	[kyrdan]

49. Restaurant

restaurant	restoran	[ræstoran]
coffee house	kahvehane	[kahvæhanæ]
pub, bar	bar	[bar]
tearoom	çay salonu	[tʃaj salonu]
waiter	garson	[garson]
waitress	kadın garson	[kadın garson]
bartender	barmen	[barmæn]
menu	menü	[mæny]
wine list	şarap listesi	[ʃarap listæsi]
to book a table	masa ayırtmak	[masa ajırtmak]
course, dish	yemek	[jæmæk]
to order (meal)	sipariş etmek	[sipariʃ ætmæk]
to make an order	sipariş vermek	[sipariʃ værmæk]
aperitif	aperatif	[apæratif]
appetizer	çerez	[tʃæræz]
dessert	tatlı	[tatlı]
check	hesap	[hæsap]
to pay the check	hesabı ödemek	[hæsabı ødæmæk]
to give change	para üstü vermek	[para justy værmæk]
tip	bahşiş	[bahʃiʃ]

50. Meals

| food | yemek | [jæmæk] |
| to eat (vi, vt) | yemek | [jæmæk] |

breakfast	kahvaltı	[kahvaltı]
to have breakfast	kahvaltı yapmak	[kahvaltı japmak]
lunch	öğle yemeği	[øjlæ jæmæi]
to have lunch	öğle yemeği yemek	[øjlæ jæmæi jæmæk]
dinner	akşam yemeği	[akʃam jæmæi]
to have dinner	akşam yemeği yemek	[akʃam jæmæi jæmæk]

| appetite | iştah | [iʃtah] |
| Enjoy your meal! | Afiyet olsun! | [afijæt olsun] |

to open (~ a bottle)	açmak	[atʃmak]
to spill (liquid)	dökmek	[døkmæk]
to spill out (vi)	dökülmek	[døkyʎmæk]

to boil (vi)	kaynamak	[kajnamak]
to boil (vt)	kaynatmak	[kajnatmak]
boiled (~ water)	kaynamış	[kajnamıʃ]
to chill, cool down (vt)	serinletmek	[særinlætmæk]
to chill (vi)	serinleşmek	[særinlæʃmæk]

| taste, flavor | tat | [tat] |
| aftertaste | ağızda kalan tat | [aızda kalan tat] |

to be on a diet	zayıflamak	[zajıflamak]
diet	rejim, diyet	[ræʒim], [dijæt]
vitamin	vitamin	[vitamin]
calorie	kalori	[kalori]
vegetarian (n)	vejetaryen kimse	[vædʒætariæn kimsæ]
vegetarian (adj)	vejetaryen	[vædʒætariæn]

fats (nutrient)	yağlar	[ja:lar]
proteins	proteinler	[protæinlær]
carbohydrates	karbonhidratlar	[karbonhidratlar]
slice (of lemon, ham)	dilim	[dilim]
piece (of cake, pie)	parça	[partʃa]
crumb (of bread)	kırıntı	[kırıntı]

51. Cooked dishes

course, dish	yemek	[jæmæk]
cuisine	mutfak	[mutfak]
recipe	yemek tarifi	[jæmæk tarifı]
portion	porsiyon	[porsijon]
salad	salata	[salata]

soup	çorba	[tʃorba]
clear soup (broth)	et suyu	[æt suju]
sandwich (bread)	sandviç	[sandvitʃ]
fried eggs	sahanda yumurta	[sahanda jumurta]
cutlet (croquette)	köfte	[køftæ]
hamburger (beefburger)	hamburger	[hamburgær]
beefsteak	biftek	[biftæk]
stew	et kızartması, rosto	[æt kızartması], [rosto]
side dish	garnitür	[garnityr]
spaghetti	spagetti	[spagætti]
mashed potatoes	patates püresi	[patatæs pyræsi]
pizza	pizza	[pizza]
porridge (oatmeal, etc.)	lâpa	[ʎapa]
omelet	omlet	[omlæt]
boiled (e.g., ~ beef)	pişmiş	[piʃmiʃ]
smoked (adj)	tütsülenmiş, füme	[tyt͡sylænmiʃ], [fymæ]
fried (adj)	kızartılmış	[kızartılmıʃ]
dried (adj)	kuru	[kuru]
frozen (adj)	dondurulmuş	[dondurulmuʃ]
pickled (adj)	turşu	[turʃu]
sweet (sugary)	tatlı	[tatlı]
salty (adj)	tuzlu	[tuzlu]
cold (adj)	soğuk	[souk]
hot (adj)	sıcak	[sıdʒak]
bitter (adj)	acı	[adʒı]
tasty (adj)	tatlı, lezzetli	[tatlı], [læzzætlı]
to cook in boiling water	kaynatmak	[kajnatmak]
to cook (dinner)	pişirmek	[piʃirmæk]
to fry (vt)	kızartmak	[kızartmak]
to heat up (food)	ısıtmak	[ısıtmak]
to salt (vt)	tuzlamak	[tuzlamak]
to pepper (vt)	biberlemek	[bibærlæmæk]
to grate (vt)	rendelemek	[rændælæmæk]
peel (n)	kabuk	[kabuk]
to peel (vt)	soymak	[sojmak]

52. Food

meat	et	[æt]
chicken	tavuk eti	[tavuk æti]
young chicken	civciv	[dʒiv dʒiv]
duck	ördek	[ørdæk]
goose	kaz	[kaz]
game	av hayvanları	[av hajvanları]

turkey	hindi	[hindi]
pork	domuz eti	[domuz æti]
veal	dana eti	[dana æti]
lamb	koyun eti	[kojun æti]
beef	sığır eti	[sıːr æti]
rabbit	tavşan eti	[tavʃan æti]

sausage (salami, etc.)	sucuk, sosis	[sudʒuk], [sosis]
vienna sausage	sosis	[sosis]
bacon	domuz pastırması	[domuz pastırması]
ham	jambon	[ʒambon]
gammon (ham)	tütsülenmiş jambon	[tytsylænmiʃ ʒambon]

pâté	ezme	[æzmæ]
liver	karaciğer	[karadʒiær]
lard	yağ	[jaː]
ground beef	kıyma	[kıjma]
tongue	dil	[diʎ]

egg	yumurta	[jumurta]
eggs	yumurtalar	[jumurtalar]
egg white	yumurta akı	[jumurta akı]
egg yolk	yumurta sarısı	[jumurta sarısı]

fish	balık	[balık]
seafood	deniz ürünleri	[dæniz jurynlæri]
caviar	havyar	[havjar]

crab	yengeç	[jæŋætʃ]
shrimp	karides	[karidæs]
oyster	istiridye	[istiridʲæ]
spiny lobster	langust	[laŋust]
octopus	ahtapot	[ahtapot]
squid	kalamar	[kalamar]

sturgeon	mersin balığı	[mærsin balıː]
salmon	som balığı	[som balıː]
halibut	pisi balığı	[pisi balıː]

cod	morina balığı	[morina balıː]
mackerel	uskumru	[uskumru]
tuna	ton balığı	[ton balıː]
eel	yılan balığı	[jılan balıː]

trout	alabalık	[alabalık]
sardine	sardalye	[sardaʎæ]
pike	turna balığı	[turna balıː]
herring	ringa	[riŋa]

bread	ekmek	[ækmæk]
cheese	peynir	[pæjnir]
sugar	şeker	[ʃækær]

salt	tuz	[tuz]
rice	pirinç	[pirintʃ]
pasta	makarna	[makarna]
noodles	erişte	[æriʃtæ]

butter	tereyağı	[tæræjaɪ]
vegetable oil	bitkisel yağ	[bitkisæʎ jaː]
sunflower oil	ayçiçeği yağı	[ajtʃitʃæɪ jaɪ]
margarine	margarin	[margarin]

| olives | zeytin | [zæjtin] |
| olive oil | zeytin yağı | [zæjtin jaɪ] |

milk	süt	[syt]
condensed milk	yoğunlaştırılmış süt	[jounlaʃtırılmıʃ syt]
yogurt	yoğurt	[jourt]
sour cream	ekşi krema	[ækʃi kræma]
cream (of milk)	süt kaymağı	[syt kajmaɪ]

| mayonnaise | mayonez | [majonæz] |
| buttercream | krema | [kræma] |

cereal grain (wheat, etc.)	tane	[tanæ]
flour	un	[un]
canned food	konserve	[konsærvæ]

cornflakes	mısır gevreği	[mısır gævræi]
honey	bal	[bal]
jam	reçel, marmelat	[rætʃæʎ], [marmælat]
chewing gum	sakız, çiklet	[sakız], [tʃiklæt]

53. Drinks

water	su	[su]
drinking water	içme suyu	[itʃmæ suju]
mineral water	maden suyu	[madæn suju]

still (adj)	gazsız	[gazsız]
carbonated (adj)	gazlı	[gazlı]
sparkling (adj)	maden	[madæn]
ice	buz	[buz]
with ice	buzlu	[buzlu]

non-alcoholic (adj)	alkolsüz	[alkoʎsyz]
soft drink	alkolsüz içki	[alkoʎsyz itʃki]
cool soft drink	soğuk meşrubat	[sojuk mæʃrubat]
lemonade	limonata	[limonata]

| liquor | alkollü içkiler | [alkolly itʃkilær] |
| wine | şarap | [ʃarap] |

| white wine | beyaz şarap | [bæjaz ʃarap] |
| red wine | kırmızı şarap | [kırmızı ʃarap] |

liqueur	likör	[likør]
champagne	şampanya	[ʃampaɲja]
vermouth	vermut	[værmut]

whisky	viski	[viski]
vodka	votka	[votka]
gin	cin	[dʒin]
cognac	konyak	[koɲjak]
rum	rom	[rom]

coffee	kahve	[kahvæ]
black coffee	siyah kahve	[sijah kahvæ]
coffee with milk	sütlü kahve	[sytly kahvæ]
cappuccino	kaymaklı kahve	[kajmaklı kahvæ]
instant coffee	hazır kahve	[hazır kahvæ]

milk	süt	[syt]
cocktail	kokteyl	[koktæjʎ]
milk shake	sütlü kokteyl	[sytly koktæjʎ]

juice	meyve suyu	[mæjvæ suju]
tomato juice	domates suyu	[domatæs suju]
orange juice	portakal suyu	[portakal suju]
freshly squeezed juice	taze meyve suyu	[tazæ mæjvæ suju]

beer	bira	[bira]
light beer	hafif bira	[hafif bira]
dark beer	siyah bira	[sijah bira]

tea	çay	[tʃaj]
black tea	siyah çay	[sijah tʃaj]
green tea	yeşil çay	[jæʃiʎ tʃaj]

54. Vegetables

| vegetables | sebze | [sæbzæ] |
| greens | yeşillik | [jæʃiʎik] |

tomato	domates	[domatæs]
cucumber	salatalık	[salatalık]
carrot	havuç	[havutʃ]
potato	patates	[patatæs]
onion	soğan	[soan]
garlic	sarımsak	[sarımsak]

| cabbage | lahana | [ʎahana] |
| cauliflower | karnabahar | [karnabahar] |

| Brussels sprouts | Brüksel lâhanası | [bryksæʎ ʎahanası] |
| broccoli | brokoli | [brokoli] |

beetroot	pancar	[pandʒar]
eggplant	patlıcan	[patlıdʒan]
zucchini	sakız kabağı	[sakız kabaı]
pumpkin	kabak	[kabak]
turnip	şalgam	[ʃalgam]

parsley	maydanoz	[majdanoz]
dill	dereotu	[dæræotu]
lettuce	yeşil salata	[jæʃiʎ salata]
celery	kereviz	[kæræviz]
asparagus	kuşkonmaz	[kuʃkonmaz]
spinach	ıspanak	[ıspanak]

pea	bezelye	[bæzæʎʲæ]
beans	bakla	[bakla]
corn (maize)	mısır	[mısır]
kidney bean	fasulye	[fasuʎʲæ]

pepper	dolma biber	[dolma bibær]
radish	turp	[turp]
artichoke	enginar	[æŋinar]

55. Fruits. Nuts

fruit	meyve	[mæjvæ]
apple	elma	[æʎma]
pear	armut	[armut]
lemon	limon	[limon]
orange	portakal	[portakal]
strawberry	çilek	[ʧilæk]

mandarin	mandalina	[mandalina]
plum	erik	[ærik]
peach	şeftali	[ʃæftali]
apricot	kayısı	[kajısı]
raspberry	ahududu	[ahududu]
pineapple	ananas	[ananas]

banana	muz	[muz]
watermelon	karpuz	[karpuz]
grape	üzüm	[juzym]
sour cherry	vişne	[viʃnæ]
sweet cherry	kiraz	[kiraz]
melon	kavun	[kavun]

| grapefruit | greypfrut | [græjpfrut] |
| avocado | avokado | [avokado] |

papaya	papaya	[papaja]
mango	mango	[maŋo]
pomegranate	nar	[nar]

redcurrant	kırmızı frenk üzümü	[kırmızı fræŋk juzymy]
blackcurrant	siyah frenk üzümü	[sijah fræŋk juzymy]
gooseberry	bektaşı üzümü	[bæktaʃı juzymy]
bilberry	yaban mersini	[jaban mærsini]
blackberry	böğürtlen	[bøjurtlæn]

raisin	kuru üzüm	[kuru juzym]
fig	incir	[indʒir]
date	hurma	[hurma]

peanut	yerfıstığı	[jærfıstı:]
almond	badem	[badæm]
walnut	ceviz	[dʒæviz]
hazelnut	fındık	[fındık]
coconut	Hindistan cevizi	[hindistan dʒævizi]
pistachios	çam fıstığı	[tʃam fıstı:]

56. Bread. Candy

confectionery (pastry)	şekerleme	[ʃækærlæmæ]
bread	ekmek	[ækmæk]
cookies	bisküvi	[biskyvi]

chocolate (n)	çikolata	[tʃikolata]
chocolate (as adj)	çikolatalı	[tʃikolatalı]
candy	şeker	[ʃækær]
cake (e.g., cupcake)	ufak kek	[ufak kæk]
cake (e.g., birthday ~)	kek, pasta	[kæk], [pasta]

| pie (e.g., apple ~) | börek | [børæk] |
| filling (for cake, pie) | iç | [itʃ] |

whole fruit jam	reçel	[rætʃæʎ]
marmalade	marmelat	[marmælat]
waffle	gofret	[gofræt]
ice-cream	dondurma	[dondurma]

57. Spices

salt	tuz	[tuz]
salty (adj)	tuzlu	[tuzlu]
to salt (vt)	tuzlamak	[tuzlamak]
black pepper	siyah biber	[sijah bibær]
red pepper	kırmızı biber	[kırmızı bibær]

| mustard | hardal | [hardal] |
| horseradish | bayırturpu | [bajırturpu] |

condiment	çeşni	[tʃæʃni]
spice	baharat	[baharat]
sauce	salça, sos	[saltʃa], [sos]
vinegar	sirke	[sirkæ]

anise	anason	[anason]
basil	fesleğen	[fæslæ:n]
cloves	karanfil	[karanfiʎ]
ginger	zencefil	[zændʒæfiʎ]
coriander	kişniş	[kiʃniʃ]
cinnamon	tarçın	[tartʃın]

sesame	susam	[susam]
bay leaf	defne yaprağı	[dæfnæ japraı]
paprika	kırmızıbiber	[kırmızı bibær]
caraway	çörek otu	[tʃoræk otu]
saffron	safran	[safran]

PERSONAL INFORMATION. FAMILY

58. Personal information. Forms

name, first name	**ad, isim**	[ad], [isim]
family name	**soyadı**	[sojadı]
date of birth	**doğum tarihi**	[doum tarihi]
place of birth	**doğum yeri**	[doum jæri]
nationality	**milliyet**	[millijæt]
place of residence	**ikamet yeri**	[ikamæt jæri]
country	**ülke**	[juʎkæ]
profession (occupation)	**meslek**	[mæslæk]
gender, sex	**cinsiyet**	[dʒinsijæt]
height	**boy**	[boj]
weight	**ağırlık**	[aırlık]

59. Family members. Relatives

mother	**anne**	[aŋæ]
father	**baba**	[baba]
son	**oğul**	[øul]
daughter	**kız**	[kız]
younger daughter	**küçük kız**	[kytʃuk kız]
younger son	**küçük oğul**	[kytʃuk oul]
eldest daughter	**büyük kız**	[byjuk kız]
eldest son	**büyük oğul**	[byjuk oul]
brother	**kardeş**	[kardæʃ]
sister	**abla**	[abla]
cousin (masc.)	**erkek kuzen**	[ærkæk kuzæn]
cousin (fem.)	**kız kuzen**	[kız kuzæn]
mom	**anne**	[aŋæ]
dad, daddy	**baba**	[baba]
parents	**ana baba**	[ana baba]
child	**çocuk**	[tʃodʒuk]
children	**çocuklar**	[tʃodʒuklar]
grandmother	**büyük anne**	[byjuk aŋæ]
grandfather	**büyük baba**	[byjuk baba]
grandson	**erkek torun**	[ærkæk torun]

granddaughter	kız torun	[kız torun]
grandchildren	torunlar	[torunlar]
uncle	amca, dayı	[amdʒa], [dai:]
aunt	teyze, hala	[tæjzæ], [hala]
nephew	erkek yeğen	[ærkæk jæ:n]
niece	kız yeğen	[kız jæ:n]
mother-in-law (wife's mother)	kaynana	[kajnana]
father-in-law (husband's father)	kaynata	[kajnata]
son-in-law (daughter's husband)	güvey	[gyvæj]
stepmother	üvey anne	[juvæj aŋæ]
stepfather	üvey baba	[juvæj baba]
infant	süt çocuğu	[syt tʃodʒu:]
baby (infant)	bebek	[bæbæk]
little boy, kid	erkek çocuk	[ærkæk tʃodʒuk]
wife	hanım, eş	[hanım], [æʃ]
husband	eş, koca	[æʃ], [kodʒa]
spouse (husband)	koca	[kodʒa]
spouse (wife)	karı	[karı]
married (masc.)	evli	[ævli]
married (fem.)	evli	[ævli]
single (unmarried)	bekâr	[bækʲar]
bachelor	bekâr	[bækʲar]
divorced (masc.)	boşanmış	[boʃanmıʃ]
widow	dul kadın	[dul kadın]
widower	dul erkek	[dul ærkæk]
relative	akraba	[akraba]
close relative	yakın akraba	[jakın akraba]
distant relative	uzak akraba	[uzak akraba]
relatives	akrabalar	[akrabalar]
orphan (boy or girl)	yetim	[jætim]
guardian (of minor)	vasi	[vasi]
to adopt (a boy)	evlatlık almak	[ævlatlık almak]
to adopt (a girl)	evlatlık almak	[ævlatlık almak]

60. Friends. Coworkers

friend (masc.)	dost, arkadaş	[dost], [arkadaʃ]
friend (fem.)	kız arkadaş	[kız arkadaʃ]
friendship	dostluk	[dostluk]
to be friends	arkadaş olmak	[arkadaʃ olmak]

buddy (masc.)	**arkadaş**	[arkadaʃ]
buddy (fem.)	**kız arkadaş**	[kız arkadaʃ]
partner	**ortak**	[ortak]
chief (boss)	**şef**	[ʃæf]
superior	**amir**	[amir]
subordinate	**ast**	[ast]
colleague	**meslektaş**	[mæslæktaʃ]
acquaintance (person)	**tanıdık**	[tanıdık]
fellow traveler	**yol arkadaşı**	[jol arkadaʃı]
classmate	**sınıf arkadaşı**	[sınıf arkadaʃı]
neighbor (masc.)	**komşu**	[komʃu]
neighbor (fem.)	**komşu**	[komʃu]
neighbors	**komşular**	[komʃular]

HUMAN BODY. MEDICINE

61. Head

head	baş	[baʃ]
face	yüz	[juz]
nose	burun	[burun]
mouth	ağız	[aız]
eye	göz	[gøz]
eyes	gözler	[gøzlær]
pupil	gözbebeği	[gøz bæbæı]
eyebrow	kaş	[kaʃ]
eyelash	kirpik	[kirpik]
eyelid	göz kapağı	[gøz kapaı]
tongue	dil	[diʎ]
tooth	diş	[diʃ]
lips	dudaklar	[dudaklar]
cheekbones	elmacık kemiği	[ælmadʒik kæmiı]
gum	dişeti	[diʃæti]
palate	damak	[damak]
nostrils	burun deliği	[burun dæliı]
chin	çene	[tʃænæ]
jaw	çene	[tʃænæ]
cheek	yanak	[janak]
forehead	alın	[alın]
temple	şakak	[ʃakak]
ear	kulak	[kulak]
back of the head	ense	[ænsæ]
neck	boyun	[bojun]
throat	boğaz	[boaz]
hair	saçlar	[satʃlar]
hairstyle	saç	[satʃ]
haircut	saç biçimi	[satʃ bitʃimi]
wig	peruk	[pæryk]
mustache	bıyık	[bıjık]
beard	sakal	[sakal]
to have (a beard, etc.)	uzatmak, bırakmak	[uzatmak], [bırakmak]
braid	saç örgüsü	[satʃ ørgysy]
sideburns	favori	[favori]
red-haired (adj)	kızıl saçlı	[kızıl satʃlı]

gray (hair)	kır	[kır]
bald (adj)	kel	[kæʎ]
bald patch	dazlak yer	[dazlak jær]

| ponytail | kuyruk | [kujruk] |
| bangs | kakül | [kakyʎ] |

62. Human body

| hand | el | [æʎ] |
| arm | kol | [kol] |

finger	parmak	[parmak]
thumb	başparmak	[baʃ parmak]
little finger	küçük parmak	[kytʃuk parmak]
nail	tırnak	[tırnak]

fist	yumruk	[jumruk]
palm	avuç	[avutʃ]
wrist	bilek	[bilæk]
forearm	önkol	[øŋkol]

| elbow | dirsek | [dirsæk] |
| shoulder | omuz | [omuz] |

leg	bacak	[badʒak]
foot	ayak	[ajak]
knee	diz	[diz]
calf (part of leg)	baldır	[baldır]

| hip | kalça | [kaltʃa] |
| heel | topuk | [topuk] |

body	vücut	[vydʒut]
stomach	karın	[karın]
chest	göğüs	[gøjus]
breast	göğüs	[gøjus]
flank	yan	[jan]
back	sırt	[sırt]

| lower back | alt bel | [alt bæʎ] |
| waist | bel | [bæʎ] |

navel	göbek	[gøbæk]
buttocks	kaba et	[kaba æt]
bottom	kıç	[kıtʃ]

beauty mark	ben	[bæn]
tattoo	dövme	[døvmæ]
scar	yara izi	[jara izi]

63. Diseases

sickness	hastalık	[hastalık]
to be sick	hasta olmak	[hasta olmak]
health	sağlık	[sa:lık]
runny nose (coryza)	nezle	[næzlæ]
angina	anjin	[anʒin]
cold (illness)	soğuk algınlığı	[souk algınlı:]
to catch a cold	soğuk almak	[souk almak]
bronchitis	bronşit	[bronʃit]
pneumonia	zatürree	[zatyræ]
flu, influenza	grip	[grip]
near-sighted (adj)	miyop	[mijop]
far-sighted (adj)	hipermetrop	[hipærmætrop]
strabismus (crossed eyes)	şaşılık	[ʃaʃılık]
cross-eyed (adj)	şaşı	[ʃaʃı]
cataract	katarakt	[katarakt]
glaucoma	glokoma	[glokoma]
stroke	felç	[fæʎtʃ]
heart attack	enfarktüs	[ænfarktys]
myocardial infarction	kalp krizi	[kaʎp krizi]
paralysis	felç	[fæʎtʃ]
to paralyze (vt)	felç olmak	[fæʎtʃ olmak]
allergy	alerji	[alærʒi]
asthma	astım	[astım]
diabetes	diyabet	[diabæt]
toothache	diş ağrısı	[diʃ a:rısı]
caries	diş çürümesi	[diʃ tʃurymæsi]
diarrhea	ishal	[ishaʎ]
constipation	kabız	[kabız]
stomach upset	mide bozukluğu	[midæ bozuklu:]
food poisoning	zehirlenme	[zæhirlænmæ]
to have a food poisoning	zehirlenmek	[zæhirlænmæk]
arthritis	artrit, arterit	[artrit]
rickets	raşitizm	[raʃitizm]
rheumatism	romatizma	[romatizma]
atherosclerosis	damar sertliği	[damar særtli:]
gastritis	gastrit	[gastrit]
appendicitis	apandisit	[apandisit]
ulcer	ülser	[juʎsær]
measles	kızamık	[kızamık]
German measles	kızamıkçık	[kızamıktʃik]

jaundice	sarılık	[sarılık]
hepatitis	hepatit	[hæpatit]
schizophrenia	şizofreni	[ʃizofræni]
rabies (hydrophobia)	kuduz hastalığı	[kuduz hastalı:]
neurosis	nevroz	[nævroz]
concussion	beyin kanaması	[bæjın kanaması]
cancer	kanser	[kansær]
sclerosis	skleroz	[sklæroz]
multiple sclerosis	multipl skleroz	[muʌtipl sklæroz]
alcoholism	alkoliklik	[alkoliklik]
alcoholic (n)	alkolik	[alkolik]
syphilis	frengi	[fræŋi]
AIDS	AİDS	[æids]
tumor	tümör, ur	[tymør], [jur]
malignant (adj)	kötü huylu	[køty hujlu]
benign (adj)	iyi huylu	[ijı hujlu]
fever	sıtma	[sıtma]
malaria	malarya	[malarja]
gangrene	kangren	[kaŋræn]
seasickness	deniz tutması	[dæniz tutması]
epilepsy	epilepsi	[æpilæpsi]
epidemic	salgın	[salgın]
typhus	tifüs	[tifys]
tuberculosis	verem	[væræm]
cholera	kolera	[kolæra]
plague (bubonic ~)	veba	[væba]

64. Symptoms. Treatments. Part 1

symptom	belirti	[bælirti]
temperature	ateş	[atæʃ]
high temperature	yüksek ateş	[juksæk atæʃ]
pulse	nabız	[nabız]
giddiness	baş dönmesi	[baʃ dønmæsi]
hot (adj)	ateşli	[atæʃli]
shivering	üşüme	[juʃymæ]
pale (e.g., ~ face)	solgun	[solgun]
cough	öksürük	[øksyryk]
to cough (vi)	öksürmek	[øksyrmæk]
to sneeze (vi)	hapşırmak	[hapʃırmak]
faint	baygınlık	[bajgınlık]
to faint (vi)	bayılmak	[bajılmak]

bruise (hématome)	çürük	[tʃuryk]
bump (lump)	şişlik	[ʃiʃlik]
to bruise oneself	çarpmak	[tʃarpmak]
bruise (contusion)	yara	[jara]
to get bruised	yaralamak	[jaralamak]

to limp (vi)	topallamak	[topallamak]
dislocation	çıkık	[tʃɪkɪk]
to dislocate (vt)	çıkmak	[tʃɪkmak]
fracture	kırık, fraktür	[kirik], [fraktyr]
to have a fracture	kırılmak	[kɪrɪlmak]

cut (e.g., paper ~)	kesik	[kæsik]
to cut oneself	bir yerini kesmek	[bir jærini kæsmæk]
bleeding	kanama	[kanama]

burn (injury)	yanık	[janɪk]
to scald oneself	yanmak	[janmak]

to prick (vt)	batırmak	[batɪrmak]
to prick oneself	batırmak	[batɪrmak]
to injure (vt)	yaralamak	[jaralamak]
injury	yara, zarar	[jara], [zarar]
wound	yara	[jara]
trauma	sarsıntı	[sarsɪntɪ]

to be delirious	sayıklamak	[sajɪklamak]
to stutter (vi)	kekelemek	[kækælæmæk]
sunstroke	güneş çarpması	[gynæʃ tʃarpmasɪ]

65. Symptoms. Treatments. Part 2

pain	acı	[adʒɪ]
splinter (in foot, etc.)	kıymık	[kɪjmɪk]

sweat (perspiration)	ter	[tær]
to sweat (perspire)	terlemek	[tærlæmæk]
vomiting	kusma	[kusma]
convulsions	kramp	[kramp]

pregnant (adj)	hamile	[hamilæ]
to be born	doğmak	[do:mak]
delivery, labor	doğum	[doum]
to deliver (~ a baby)	doğurmak	[dourmak]
abortion	çocuk düşürme	[tʃodʒuk dyʃyrmæ]

breathing, respiration	respirasyon	[ræspirasʲon]
inhalation	soluk alma	[soluk alma]
exhalation	soluk verme	[soluk vermæ]
to exhale (vi)	soluk vermek	[soluk værmæk]

to inhale (vi)	bir soluk almak	[bir soluk almak]
disabled person	malul	[malyl]
cripple	sakat	[sakat]
drug addict	uyuşturucu bağımlısı	[ujuʃturudʒu baımlısı]

deaf (adj)	sağır	[saır]
dumb, mute	dilsiz	[diʎsiz]
deaf-and-dumb (adj)	sağır ve dilsiz	[saır væ diʎsiz]

mad, insane (adj)	deli	[dæli]
madman	deli adam	[dæli adam]
madwoman	deli kadın	[dæli kadın]
to go insane	çıldırmak	[tʃıldırmak]

gene	gen	[gæn]
immunity	bağışıklık	[baıʃıklık]
hereditary (adj)	irsi, kalıtsal	[irsi], [kalıtsal]
congenital (adj)	doğuştan	[douʃtan]

virus	virüs	[virys]
microbe	mikrop	[mikrop]
bacterium	bakteri	[baktæri]
infection	enfeksiyon	[ænfæksijon]

66. Symptoms. Treatments. Part 3

| hospital | hastane | [hastanæ] |
| patient | hasta | [hasta] |

diagnosis	teşhis	[tæʃhis]
cure	çare	[tʃaræ]
medical treatment	tedavi	[tædavi]
to get treatment	tedavi görmek	[tædavi gørmæk]
to treat (vt)	tedavi etmek	[tædavi ætmæk]
to nurse (look after)	hastaya bakmak	[hastaja bakmak]
care (nursing ~)	hasta bakımı	[hasta bakımı]

operation, surgery	ameliyat	[amælijat]
to bandage (head, limb)	pansuman yapmak	[pansuman japmak]
bandaging	pansuman	[pansuman]

vaccination	aşılama	[aʃılama]
to vaccinate (vt)	aşı yapmak	[aʃı japmak]
injection, shot	iğne	[i:næ]
to give an injection	iğne yapmak	[i:næ japmak]

amputation	ampütasyon	[ampytasʲon]
to amputate (vt)	ameliyatla almak	[amælijatla almak]
coma	koma	[koma]
to be in a coma	komada olmak	[komada olmak]

intensive care	yoğun bakım	[joun bakım]
to recover (~ from flu)	iyileşmek	[ijılæʃmæk]
state (patient's ~)	durum	[durum]
consciousness	bilinç	[bilintʃ]
memory (faculty)	hafıza	[hafıza]

to extract (tooth)	çekmek	[tʃækmæk]
filling	dolgu	[dolgu]
to fill (a tooth)	dolgu yapmak	[dolgu japmak]

| hypnosis | hipnoz | [hipnoz] |
| to hypnotize (vt) | hipnotize etmek | [hipnotizæ ætmæk] |

67. Medicine. Drugs. Accessories

medicine, drug	ilaç	[ilatʃ]
remedy	deva	[dæva]
to prescribe (vt)	yazmak	[jazmak]
prescription	reçete	[rætʃætæ]

tablet, pill	hap	[hap]
ointment	merhem	[mærhæm]
ampule	ampul	[ampuʎ]
mixture	solüsyon	[solysʲon]
syrup	şurup	[ʃurup]
pill	kapsül	[kapsyl]
powder	toz	[toz]

bandage	bandaj	[bandaʒ]
cotton wool	pamuk	[pamuk]
iodine	iyot	[ijot]

Band-Aid	yara bandı	[jara bandı]
eyedropper	damlalık	[damlalık]
thermometer	derece	[dærædʒæ]
syringe	şırınga	[ʃiriŋa]

| wheelchair | tekerlekli sandalye | [tækærlækli sandaʎʲæ] |
| crutches | koltuk değneği | [koltuk dæjnæi] |

painkiller	anestetik	[anæstætik]
laxative	müshil	[myshiʎ]
spirit (ethanol)	ispirto	[ispirto]
medicinal herbs	şifalı bitkiler	[ʃifalı bitkilær]
herbal (~ tea)	bitkisel	[bitkisæʎ]

APARTMENT

68. Apartment

apartment	daire	[dairæ]
room	oda	[oda]
bedroom	yatak odası	[jatak odası]
dining room	yemek odası	[jæmæk odası]
living room	misafir odası	[misafir odası]
study (home office)	çalışma odası	[tʃalıʃma odası]
entry room	antre	[antræ]
bathroom	banyo odası	[baɲʲo odası]
half bath	tuvalet	[tuvalæt]
ceiling	tavan	[tavan]
floor	taban, yer	[taban], [jær]
corner	köşesi	[køʃæsi]

69. Furniture. Interior

furniture	mobilya	[mobiʎja]
table	masa	[masa]
chair	sandalye	[sandaʎʲæ]
bed	yatak	[jatak]
couch, sofa	kanape	[kanapæ]
armchair	koltuk	[koltuk]
bookcase	kitaplık	[kitaplık]
shelf	kitap rafı	[kitap rafı]
set of shelves	etajer	[ætaʒær]
wardrobe	elbise dolabı	[æʎbisæ dolabı]
coat rack	duvar askısı	[duvar askısı]
coat stand	portmanto	[portmanto]
dresser	komot	[komot]
coffee table	sehpa	[sæhpa]
mirror	ayna	[ajna]
carpet	halı	[halı]
rug, small carpet	kilim	[kilim]
fireplace	şömine	[ʃominæ]
candle	mum	[mum]

candlestick	mumluk	[mumluk]
drapes	perdeler	[pærdlær]
wallpaper	duvar kağıdı	[duvar k'aıdı]
blinds (jalousie)	jaluzi	[ʒalyzi]
table lamp	masa lambası	[masa lambası]
wall lamp (sconce)	lamba	[lamba]
floor lamp	ayaklı lamba	[ajaklı lamba]
chandelier	avize	[avizæ]
leg (of chair, table)	ayak	[ajak]
armrest	kol	[kol]
back (backrest)	arkalık	[arkalık]
drawer	çekmece	[ʧækmæʤæ]

70. Bedding

bedclothes	çamaşır	[ʧamaʃır]
pillow	yastık	[jastık]
pillowcase	yastık kılıfı	[jastık kılıfı]
blanket (comforter)	battaniye	[battanijæ]
sheet	çarşaf	[ʧarʃaf]
bedspread	örtü	[ørty]

71. Kitchen

kitchen	mutfak	[mutfak]
gas	gaz	[gaz]
gas cooker	gaz sobası	[gaz sobası]
electric cooker	elektrik ocağı	[ælæktrik oʤaı]
oven	fırın	[fırın]
microwave oven	mikrodalga fırın	[mikrodalga fırın]
refrigerator	buzdolabı	[buzdolabı]
freezer	derin dondurucu	[dærin donduruʤu]
dishwasher	bulaşık makinesi	[bulaʃık makinæsi]
meat grinder	kıyma makinesi	[kıjma makinæsi]
juicer	meyve sıkacağı	[mæjvæ sıkaʤaı]
toaster	tost makinesi	[tost makinæsi]
mixer	mikser	[miksær]
coffee maker	kahve makinesi	[kahvæ makinæsi]
coffee pot	cezve	[ʤæzvæ]
coffee grinder	kahve değirmeni	[kahvæ dæirmæni]
kettle	çaydanlık	[ʧajdanlık]
teapot	demlik	[dæmlik]

| lid | kapak | [kapak] |
| tea strainer | süzgeci | [syzgædʒi] |

spoon	kaşık	[kaʃık]
teaspoon	çay kaşığı	[tʃaj kaʃı:]
tablespoon	yemek kaşığı	[jæmæk kaʃı:]
fork	çatal	[tʃatal]
knife	bıçak	[bıtʃak]

tableware (dishes)	mutfak gereçleri	[mutfak gærætʃlæri]
plate (dinner ~)	tabak	[tabak]
saucer	fincan tabağı	[findʒan tabaı]

shot glass	kadeh	[kadæ]
glass (~ of water)	bardak	[bardak]
cup	fincan	[findʒan]

sugar bowl	şekerlik	[ʃækærlik]
salt shaker	tuzluk	[tuzluk]
pepper shaker	biberlik	[bibærlik]
butter dish	tereyağı tabağı	[tæræjaı tabaı]

saucepan	tencere	[tændʒæræ]
frying pan	tava	[tava]
ladle	kepçe	[kæptʃæ]
colander	süzgeç	[syzgætʃ]
tray	tepsi	[tæpsi]

bottle	şişe	[ʃiʃæ]
jar (glass)	kavanoz	[kavanoz]
can	teneke	[tænækæ]

bottle opener	şişe açacağı	[ʃiʃæ atʃadʒaı]
can opener	konserve açacağı	[konsærvæ atʃadʒaı]
corkscrew	tirbuşon	[tirbyʃon]
filter	filtre	[fiʌtræ]
to filter (vt)	filtre etmek	[fiʌtræ ætmæk]

| trash | çöp | [tʃop] |
| trash can | çöp kovası | [tʃop kovası] |

72. Bathroom

bathroom	banyo odası	[baɲ'o odası]
water	su	[su]
tap, faucet	musluk	[musluk]
hot water	sıcak su	[sıdʒak su]
cold water	soğuk su	[souk su]
toothpaste	diş macunu	[diʃ madʒunu]
to brush one's teeth	dişlerini fırçalamak	[diʃlærini fırtʃalamak]

T&P Books. Turkish vocabulary for English speakers - 3000 words

to shave (vi)	tıraş olmak	[tıraʃ olmak]
shaving foam	tıraş köpüğü	[tıraʃ køpyju]
razor	jilet	[ʒilæt]

to wash (one's hands, etc.)	yıkamak	[jıkamak]
to take a bath	yıkanmak	[jıkanmak]
shower	duş	[duʃ]
to take a shower	duş almak	[duʃ almak]

bathtub	banyo	[baɲʲo]
toilet (toilet bowl)	klozet	[klozæt]
sink (washbasin)	küvet	[kyvæt]

| soap | sabun | [sabun] |
| soap dish | sabunluk | [sabunluk] |

sponge	sünger	[syŋær]
shampoo	şampuan	[ʃampuan]
towel	havlu	[havlu]
bathrobe	bornoz	[bornoz]

laundry (process)	çamaşır yıkama	[tʃamaʃır jıkama]
washing machine	çamaşır makinesi	[tʃamaʃır makinæsi]
to do the laundry	çamaşırları yıkamak	[tʃamaʃırları jıkamak]
laundry detergent	çamaşır deterjanı	[tʃamaʃır dætærʒanı]

73. Household appliances

TV set	televizyon	[tælævizʲon]
tape recorder	teyp	[tæjp]
video, VCR	video	[vidæo]
radio	radyo	[radʲo]
player (CD, MP3, etc.)	çalar	[tʃalar]

video projector	projeksiyon makinesi	[proʒæksion makinæsi]
home movie theater	ev sinema	[ævʲ sinæma]
DVD player	DVD oynatıcı	[dividi ojnatıdʒı]
amplifier	amplifikatör	[amplifikator]
video game console	oyun konsolu	[ojun konsolu]

video camera	video kamera	[vidæokamæra]
camera (photo)	fotoğraf makinesi	[fotoraf makinæsi]
digital camera	dijital fotoğraf makinesi	[diʒital fotoraf makinæsi]

vacuum cleaner	elektrik süpürgesi	[ælæktrik sypyrgæsi]
iron (e.g., steam ~)	ütü	[juty]
ironing board	ütü masası	[juty masası]

| telephone | telefon | [tælæfon] |
| mobile phone | cep telefonu | [dʒæp tælæfonu] |

typewriter	daktilo	[daktilo]
sewing machine	dikiş makinesi	[dikiʃ makinæsi]
microphone	mikrofon	[mikrofon]
headphones	kulaklık	[kulaklık]
remote control (TV)	uzaktan kumanda	[uzaktan kumanda]
CD, compact disc	CD	[sidi]
cassette	teyp kaseti	[tæjp kasæti]
vinyl record	vinil plak	[vinil plak]

THE EARTH. WEATHER

74. Outer space

cosmos	uzay, evren	[uzaj], [ævræn]
space (as adj)	uzay	[uzaj]
outer space	feza	[fæza]
world	kainat	[kajnat]
universe	evren	[ævræn]
galaxy	galaksi	[galaksi]
star	yıldız	[jıldız]
constellation	takımyıldız	[takımjıldız]
planet	gezegen	[gæzægæn]
satellite	uydu	[ujdu]
meteorite	göktaşı	[gøktaʃı]
comet	kuyruklu yıldız	[kujruklu jıldız]
asteroid	asteroit	[astæroit]
orbit	yörünge	[joryŋæ]
to revolve (~ around the Earth)	dönmek	[dønmæk]
atmosphere	atmosfer	[atmosfær]
the Sun	Güneş	[gynæʃ]
solar system	Güneş sistemi	[gynæʃ sistæmi]
solar eclipse	Güneş tutulması	[gynæʃ tutulması]
the Earth	Dünya	[dyɲja]
the Moon	Ay	[aj]
Mars	Mars	[mars]
Venus	Venüs	[vænys]
Jupiter	Jüpiter	[ʒupitær]
Saturn	Satürn	[satyrn]
Mercury	Merkür	[mærkyr]
Uranus	Uranüs	[uranys]
Neptune	Neptün	[næptyn]
Pluto	Plüton	[plyton]
Milky Way	Samanyolu	[samaɲjolu]
Great Bear	Büyükayı	[byjuk ajı]
North Star	Kutup yıldızı	[kutup jıldızı]
Martian	Merihli	[mærihli]

extraterrestrial (n)	uzaylı	[uzajlı]
alien	uzaylı	[uzajlı]
flying saucer	uçan daire	[utʃan dairæ]

spaceship	uzay gemisi	[uzaj gæmisi]
space station	yörünge istasyonu	[joryŋæ istasʲonu]
blast-off	uzaya fırlatma	[uzaja fırlatma]

engine	motor	[motor]
nozzle	roket meme	[rokæt mæmæ]
fuel	yakıt	[jakıt]

cockpit, flight deck	kabin	[kabin]
antenna	anten	[antæn]
porthole	lombar	[lombar]
solar battery	güneş pili	[gynæʃ pili]
spacesuit	uzay elbisesi	[uzaj æʎbisæsi]

weightlessness	ağırlıksızlık	[aırlıksızlık]
oxygen	oksijen	[oksiʒæn]

docking (in space)	uzayda kenetlenme	[uzajda kænætlænmæ]
to dock (vi, vt)	kenetlenmek	[kænætlænmæk]

observatory	gözlemevi	[gøzlæmævi]
telescope	teleskop	[tælæskop]
to observe (vt)	gözlemlemek	[gøzlæmlæmæk]
to explore (vt)	araştırmak	[araʃtırmak]

75. The Earth

the Earth	Dünya	[dyɲja]
globe (the Earth)	yerküre	[jærkyræ]
planet	gezegen	[gæzægæn]

atmosphere	atmosfer	[atmosfær]
geography	coğrafya	[dʒorafja]
nature	doğa	[doa]

globe (table ~)	yerküre	[jærkyræ]
map	harita	[harita]
atlas	atlas	[atlas]

Europe	Avrupa	[avrupa]
Asia	Asya	[asja]
Africa	Afrika	[afrika]
Australia	Avustralya	[avustraʎja]

America	Amerika	[amærika]
North America	Kuzey Amerika	[kuzæj amærika]

South America	Güney Amerika	[gynæj amærika]
Antarctica	Antarktik	[antarktik]
the Arctic	Arktik	[arktik]

76. Cardinal directions

north	kuzey	[kuzæj]
to the north	kuzeye	[kuzæjæ]
in the north	kuzeyde	[kuzæjdæ]
northern (adj)	kuzey	[kuzæj]

south	güney	[gynæj]
to the south	güneye	[gynæjæ]
in the south	güneyde	[gynæjdæ]
southern (adj)	güney	[gynæj]

west	batı	[batı]
to the west	batıya	[batıja]
in the west	batıda	[batıda]
western (adj)	batı	[batı]

east	doğu	[dou]
to the east	doğuya	[douja]
in the east	doğuda	[douda]
eastern (adj)	doğu	[dou]

77. Sea. Ocean

sea	deniz	[dæniz]
ocean	okyanus	[okjanus]
gulf (bay)	körfez	[kørfæz]
straits	boğaz	[boaz]

continent (mainland)	kıta	[kıta]
island	ada	[ada]
peninsula	yarımada	[jarımada]
archipelago	takımada	[takımada]

bay, cove	koy	[koj]
harbor	liman	[liman]
lagoon	deniz kulağı	[dæniz kulaı]
cape	burun	[burun]

atoll	atol	[atol]
reef	resif	[ræsif]
coral	mercan	[mærdʒan]
coral reef	mercan kayalığı	[mærdʒan kajalı:]
deep (adj)	derin	[dærin]

depth (deep water)	derinlik	[dærinlik]
abyss	uçurum	[utʃurum]
trench (e.g., Mariana ~)	çukur	[tʃukur]
current, stream	akıntı	[akıntı]
to surround (bathe)	çevrelemek	[tʃævrælæmæk]
shore	kıyı	[kıjı]
coast	kıyı, sahil	[kıjı], [sahil]
high tide	kabarma	[kabarma]
low tide	cezir	[dʒæzir]
sandbank	sığlık	[sıːlık]
bottom	dip	[dip]
wave	dalga	[dalga]
crest (~ of a wave)	dağ sırtı	[daı sırtı]
froth (foam)	köpük	[køpyk]
storm	fırtına	[fırtına]
hurricane	kasırga	[kasırga]
tsunami	tsunami	[tsunami]
calm (dead ~)	limanlık	[limanlık]
quiet, calm (adj)	sakin	[sakin]
pole	kutup	[kutup]
polar (adj)	kutuplu	[kutuplu]
latitude	enlem	[ænlæm]
longitude	boylam	[bojlam]
parallel	paralel	[paralæʎ]
equator	ekvator	[ækvator]
sky	gök	[gøk]
horizon	ufuk	[ufuk]
air	hava	[hava]
lighthouse	deniz feneri	[dæniz fænæri]
to dive (vi)	dalmak	[dalmak]
to sink (ab. boat)	batmak	[batmak]
treasures	hazine	[hazinæ]

78. Seas' and Oceans' names

Atlantic Ocean	Atlas Okyanusu	[atlas okjanusu]
Indian Ocean	Hint Okyanusu	[hint okjanusu]
Pacific Ocean	Pasifik Okyanusu	[pasifik okjanusu]
Arctic Ocean	Kuzey Buz Denizi	[kuzæj buz dænizi]
Black Sea	Karadeniz	[karadæniz]
Red Sea	Kızıldeniz	[kızıldæniz]

Yellow Sea	Sarı Deniz	[sarı dæniz]
White Sea	Beyaz Deniz	[bæjaz dæniz]
Caspian Sea	Hazar Denizi	[hazar dænizi]
Dead Sea	Ölüdeniz	[ølydæniz]
Mediterranean Sea	Akdeniz	[akdæniz]
Aegean Sea	Ege Denizi	[ægæ dænizi]
Adriatic Sea	Adriyatik Denizi	[adrijatik dænizi]
Arabian Sea	Umman Denizi	[umman dænizi]
Sea of Japan	Japon Denizi	[ʒapon dænizi]
Bering Sea	Bering Denizi	[bæriŋ dænizi]
South China Sea	Güney Çin Denizi	[gynæj tʃin dænizi]
Coral Sea	Mercan Denizi	[mærdʒan dænizi]
Tasman Sea	Tasman Denizi	[tasman dænizi]
Caribbean Sea	Karayip Denizi	[karaip dænizi]
Barents Sea	Barents Denizi	[barænts dænizi]
Kara Sea	Kara Denizi	[kara dænizi]
North Sea	Kuzey Denizi	[kuzæj dænizi]
Baltic Sea	Baltık Denizi	[baltık dænizi]
Norwegian Sea	Norveç Denizi	[norvætʃ dænizi]

79. Mountains

mountain	dağ	[da:]
mountain range	dağ silsilesi	[da: silsilæsi]
mountain ridge	sıradağlar	[sırada:lar]
summit, top	zirve	[zirvæ]
peak	doruk, zirve	[doruk], [zirvæ]
foot (of mountain)	etek	[ætæk]
slope (mountainside)	yamaç	[jamatʃ]
volcano	yanardağ	[janarda:]
active volcano	faal yanardağ	[fa:ʎ janarda:]
dormant volcano	sönmüş yanardağ	[sønmyʃ janarda:]
eruption	püskürme	[pyskyrmæ]
crater	yanardağ ağzı	[janarda: a:zı]
magma	magma	[magma]
lava	lav	[lav]
molten (~ lava)	kızgın	[kızgın]
canyon	kanyon	[kaɲʲon]
gorge	boğaz	[boaz]
crevice	dere	[dæræ]

abyss (chasm)	uçurum	[utʃurum]
pass, col	dağ geçidi	[da: gætʃidi]
plateau	yayla	[jajla]
cliff	kaya	[kaja]
hill	tepe	[tæpæ]
glacier	buzluk	[buzluk]
waterfall	şelâle	[ʃælalæ]
geyser	gayzer	[gajzær]
lake	göl	[gøʎ]
plain	ova	[ova]
landscape	manzara	[manzara]
echo	yankı	[jaŋkı]
alpinist	dağcı, alpinist	[da:dʒı], [alpinist]
rock climber	dağcı	[da:dʒı]
to conquer (in climbing)	fethetmek	[fæthætmæk]
climb (an easy ~)	tırmanma	[tırmanma]

80. Mountains names

Alps	Alp Dağları	[aʎp da:ları]
Mont Blanc	Mont Blanc	[mont blan]
Pyrenees	Pireneler	[pirinælær]
Carpathians	Karpatlar	[karpatlar]
Ural Mountains	Ural Dağları	[ural da:ları]
Caucasus	Kafkasya	[kafkasja]
Elbrus	Elbruz Dağı	[ælbrus da:ı]
Altai	Altay	[altaj]
Tien Shan	Tien-şan	[tʲæn ʃan]
Pamir Mountains	Pamir	[pamir]
Himalayas	Himalaya Dağları	[himalaja da:ları]
Everest	Everest Dağı	[æværæst da:ı]
Andes	And Dağları	[and da:ları]
Kilimanjaro	Kilimanjaro	[kilimandʒaro]

81. Rivers

river	nehir, ırmak	[næhir], [ırmak]
spring (natural source)	kaynak	[kajnak]
riverbed	nehir yatağı	[næhir jataı]
basin	havza	[havza]
to flow into ...	... dökülmek	[døkyʎmæk]
tributary	kol	[kol]

bank (of river)	sahil	[sahiʎ]
current, stream	akıntı	[akıntı]
downstream (adv)	nehir boyunca	[næhir bojundʒa]
upstream (adv)	nehirden yukarı	[næhirdæn jukarı]
inundation	taşkın	[taʃkın]
flooding	nehrin taşması	[næhrin taʃması]
to overflow (vi)	taşmak	[taʃmak]
to flood (vt)	su basmak	[su basmak]
shallows (shoal)	sığlık	[sıːlık]
rapids	nehrin akıntılı yeri	[næhrin akıntılı jæri]
dam	baraj	[baraʒ]
canal	kanal	[kanal]
artificial lake	baraj gölü	[baraʒ gøly]
sluice, lock	alavere havuzu	[alaværæ havuzu]
water body (pond, etc.)	su birikintisi	[su birikintisi]
swamp, bog	bataklık	[bataklık]
marsh	bataklık arazi	[bataklık arazi]
whirlpool	girdap	[girdap]
stream (brook)	dere	[dæræ]
drinking (ab. water)	içilir	[itʃilir]
fresh (~ water)	tatlı	[tatlı]
ice	buz	[buz]
to freeze (ab. river, etc.)	buz tutmak	[buz tutmak]

82. Rivers' names

Seine	Sen nehri	[sæn næhri]
Loire	Loire nehri	[luara næhri]
Thames	Thames nehri	[tæmz næhri]
Rhine	Ren nehri	[ræn næhri]
Danube	Tuna nehri	[tuna næhri]
Volga	Volga nehri	[volga næhri]
Don	Don nehri	[don næhri]
Lena	Lena nehri	[læna næhri]
Yellow River	Sarı Irmak	[sarı ırmak]
Yangtze	Yangçe nehri	[jantʃæ næhri]
Mekong	Mekong nehri	[mækoŋ næhri]
Ganges	Ganj nehri	[ganʒ næhri]
Nile River	Nil nehri	[nil næhri]
Congo	Kongo nehri	[koŋo næhri]

Okavango	Okavango nehri	[okavaŋo næhri]
Zambezi	Zambezi nehri	[zambæzi næhri]
Limpopo	Limpopo nehri	[limpopo næhri]
Mississippi River	Mississippi nehri	[misisipi næhri]

83. Forest

| forest | orman | [orman] |
| forest (as adj) | orman | [orman] |

thick forest	kesif orman	[kæsif orman]
grove	koru, ağaçlık	[koru], [a:tʃlık]
forest clearing	ormanda açıklığı	[ormanda atʃıklı:]

| thicket | sık ağaçlık | [ʃık a:tʃlık] |
| scrubland | çalılık | [tʃalılık] |

| footpath (troddenpath) | keçi yolu | [kætʃi jolu] |
| gully | sel yatağı | [sæl jataı] |

tree	ağaç	[a:tʃ]
leaf	yaprak	[japrak]
leaves	yapraklar	[japraklar]

fall of leaves	yaprak dökümü	[japrak døkymy]
to fall (ab. leaves)	dökülmek	[døkyʎmæk]
top (of the tree)	ağacın tepesi	[a:dʒin tæpæsi]

branch	dal	[dal]
bough	ağaç dalı	[a:tʃ dalı]
bud (on shrub, tree)	tomurcuk	[tomurdʒuk]
needle (of pine tree)	iğne yaprak	[i:næ japrak]
pine cone	kozalak	[kozalak]

hollow (in a tree)	kovuk	[kovuk]
nest	yuva	[juva]
burrow (animal hole)	in	[in]

trunk	gövde	[gøvdæ]
root	kök	[køk]
bark	kabuk	[kabuk]
moss	yosun	[josun]

to uproot (vt)	kökünden sökmek	[køkyndæn søkmæk]
to chop down	kesmek	[kæsmæk]
to deforest (vt)	ağaçları yok etmek	[a:tʃları jok ætmæk]
tree stump	kütük	[kytyk]

| campfire | kamp ateşi | [kamp atæʃi] |
| forest fire | yangın | [jaŋın] |

to extinguish (vt)	söndürmek	[søndyrmæk]
forest ranger	orman bekçisi	[orman bæktʃisi]
protection	koruma	[koruma]
to protect (~ nature)	korumak	[korumak]
poacher	kaçak avcı	[katʃak avdʒı]
trap (e.g., bear ~)	kapan	[kapan]
to gather, to pick (vt)	toplamak	[toplamak]
to lose one's way	yolunu kaybetmek	[jolunu kajbætmæk]

84. Natural resources

natural resources	doğal kaynaklar	[doal kajnaklar]
minerals	madensel maddeler	[madænsæl maddælær]
deposits	katman	[katman]
field (e.g., oilfield)	yatak	[jatak]
to mine (extract)	çıkarmak	[tʃıkarmak]
mining (extraction)	maden çıkarma	[madæn tʃikarma]
ore	filiz	[filiz]
mine (e.g., for coal)	maden ocağı	[madæn odʒaı]
mine shaft, pit	kuyu	[kuju]
miner	maden işçisi	[madæn iʃtʃisi]
gas	gaz	[gaz]
gas pipeline	gaz boru hattı	[gaz boru hattı]
oil (petroleum)	petrol	[pætrol]
oil pipeline	petrol boru hattı	[pætrol boru hattı]
oil well	petrol kulesi	[pætrol kulæsi]
derrick	sondaj kulesi	[sondaʒ kulæsi]
tanker	tanker	[taŋkær]
sand	kum	[kum]
limestone	kireçtaşı	[kirætʃtaʃi]
gravel	çakıl	[tʃakılı]
peat	turba	[turba]
clay	kil	[kiʎ]
coal	kömür	[kømyr]
iron	demir	[dæmir]
gold	altın	[altın]
silver	gümüş	[gymyʃ]
nickel	nikel	[nikæʎ]
copper	bakır	[bakır]
zinc	çinko	[tʃinko]
manganese	manganez	[maŋanæz]
mercury	cıva	[dʒıva]
lead	kurşun	[kurʃun]

mineral	mineral	[minæral]
crystal	billur	[billyr]
marble	mermer	[mærmær]
uranium	uranyum	[uraɲʲum]

85. Weather

weather	hava	[hava]
weather forecast	hava tahmini	[hava tahmini]
temperature	sıcaklık	[sɪdʒaklık]
thermometer	termometre	[tærmomætræ]
barometer	barometre	[baromætræ]
humidity	nem	[næm]
heat (extreme ~)	sıcaklık	[sɪdʒaklık]
hot (torrid)	sıcak	[sɪdʒak]
it's hot	hava sıcak	[hava sɪdʒak]
it's warm	hava ılık	[hava ılık]
warm (moderately hot)	ılık	[ılık]
it's cold	hava soğuk	[hava souk]
cold (adj)	soğuk	[souk]
sun	güneş	[gynæʃ]
to shine (vi)	ışık vermek	[ıʃık værmæk]
sunny (day)	güneşli	[gynæʃli]
to come up (vi)	doğmak	[do:mak]
to set (vi)	batmak	[batmak]
cloud	bulut	[bulut]
cloudy (adj)	bulutlu	[bulutlu]
rain cloud	yağmur bulutu	[ja:mur bulutu]
somber (gloomy)	kapalı	[kapalı]
rain	yağmur	[ja:mur]
it's raining	yağmur yağıyor	[ja:mur jaıjor]
rainy (day)	yağmurlu	[ja:murlu]
to drizzle (vi)	çiselemek	[tʃisælæmæk]
pouring rain	sağanak	[sa:nak]
downpour	şiddetli yağmur	[ʃiddætli ja:mur]
heavy (e.g., ~ rain)	şiddetli, zorlu	[ʃiddætli], [zorlu]
puddle	su birikintisi	[su birikintisi]
to get wet (in rain)	ıslanmak	[ıslanmak]
fog (mist)	sis, duman	[sis], [duman]
foggy	sisli	[sisli]
snow	kar	[kar]
it's snowing	kar yağıyor	[kar jaıjor]

86. Severe weather. Natural disasters

thunderstorm	fırtına	[fırtına]
lightning (~ strike)	şimşek	[ʃimʃæk]
to flash (vi)	çakmak	[tʃakmak]
thunder	gök gürültüsü	[gøk gyryltysy]
to thunder (vi)	gürlemek	[gyrlæmæk]
it's thundering	gök gürlüyor	[gøk gyrlyjor]
hail	dolu	[dolu]
it's hailing	dolu yağıyor	[dolu jaıjor]
to flood (vt)	su basmak	[su basmak]
flood, inundation	taşkın	[taʃkın]
earthquake	deprem	[dæpræm]
tremor, quake	sarsıntı	[sarsıntı]
epicenter	deprem merkezi	[dæpræm mærkæzi]
eruption	püskürme	[pyskyrmæ]
lava	lav	[lav]
twister	hortum	[hortum]
tornado	kasırga	[kasırga]
typhoon	tayfun	[tajfun]
hurricane	kasırga	[kasırga]
storm	fırtına	[fırtına]
tsunami	tsunami	[tsunami]
cyclone	siklon	[siklon]
bad weather	kötü hava	[køty hava]
fire (accident)	yangın	[jaŋın]
disaster	felaket	[fæʎakæt]
meteorite	göktaşı	[gøktaʃı]
avalanche	çığ	[tʃı:]
snowslide	çığ	[tʃı:]
blizzard	tipi	[tipi]
snowstorm	kar fırtınası	[kar fırtınası]

FAUNA

87. Mammals. Predators

predator	yırtıcı hayvan	[jɪrtɪʤɪ hajvan]
tiger	kaplan	[kaplan]
lion	aslan	[aslan]
wolf	kurt	[kurt]
fox	tilki	[tiʎki]

jaguar	jagar, jaguar	[ʒagar]
leopard	leopar	[læopar]
cheetah	çita	[ʧita]

black panther	panter	[pantær]
puma	puma	[puma]
snow leopard	kar leoparı	[kar læoparı]
lynx	vaşak	[vaʃak]

coyote	kır kurdu	[kır kurdu]
jackal	çakal	[ʧakal]
hyena	sırtlan	[sırtlan]

88. Wild animals

| animal | hayvan | [hajvan] |
| beast (animal) | vahşi hayvan | [vahʃi hajvan] |

squirrel	sincap	[sinʤap]
hedgehog	kirpi	[kirpi]
hare	yabani tavşan	[jabani tavʃan]
rabbit	tavşan	[tavʃan]

badger	porsuk	[porsuk]
raccoon	rakun	[rakun]
hamster	cırlak sıçan	[ʤirlak sıʧan]
marmot	dağ sıçanı	[da: sıʧanı]

mole	köstebek	[køstæbæk]
mouse	fare	[faræ]
rat	sıçan	[sıʧan]
bat	yarasa	[jarasa]
ermine	kakım	[kakım]
sable	samur	[samur]

marten	ağaç sansarı	[a:tʃ sansarı]
weasel	gelincik	[gælindʒik]
mink	vizon	[vizon]
beaver	kunduz	[kunduz]
otter	su samuru	[su samuru]
horse	at	[at]
moose	Avrupa musu	[avrupa musu]
deer	geyik	[gæjık]
camel	deve	[dævæ]
bison	bizon	[bizon]
aurochs	Avrupa bizonu	[avrupa bizonu]
buffalo	manda	[manda]
zebra	zebra	[zæbra]
antelope	antilop	[antilop]
roe deer	karaca	[karadʒa]
fallow deer	alageyik	[alagæjık]
chamois	dağ keçisi	[da: kætʃisi]
wild boar	yaban domuzu	[jaban domuzu]
whale	balina	[balina]
seal	fok	[fok]
walrus	mors	[mors]
fur seal	kürklü fok balığı	[kyrkly fok balı:]
dolphin	yunus	[junus]
bear	ayı	[ajı]
polar bear	beyaz ayı	[bæjaz ajı]
panda	panda	[panda]
monkey	maymun	[majmun]
chimpanzee	şempanze	[ʃæmpanzæ]
orangutan	orangutan	[oraŋutan]
gorilla	goril	[goriʎ]
macaque	makak	[makak]
gibbon	jibon	[ʒibon]
elephant	fil	[fiʎ]
rhinoceros	gergedan	[gærgædan]
giraffe	zürafa	[zyrafa]
hippopotamus	su aygırı	[su ajgırı]
kangaroo	kanguru	[kaŋuru]
koala (bear)	koala	[koala]
mongoose	firavunfaresi	[fıravunfaræsi]
chinchilla	şinşilla	[ʃinʃilla]
skunk	kokarca	[kokardʒa]
porcupine	oklukirpi	[oklukirpi]

89. Domestic animals

cat	kedi	[kædi]
tomcat	erkek kedi	[ærkæk kædi]

horse	at	[at]
stallion	aygır	[ajgır]
mare	kısrak	[kısrak]

cow	inek	[inæk]
bull	boğa	[boa]
ox	öküz	[økyz]

sheep	koyun	[kojun]
ram	koç	[kotʃ]
goat	keçi	[kætʃi]
billy goat, he-goat	teke	[tækæ]

donkey	eşek	[æʃæk]
mule	katır	[katır]

pig	domuz	[domuz]
piglet	domuz yavrusu	[domuz javrusu]
rabbit	tavşan	[tavʃan]

hen (chicken)	tavuk	[tavuk]
rooster	horoz	[horoz]

duck	ördek	[ørdæk]
drake	suna	[suna]
goose	kaz	[kaz]

tom turkey	erkek hindi	[ærkæk hindi]
turkey (hen)	dişi hindi	[diʃi hindi]

domestic animals	evcil hayvanlar	[ævdʒiʎ hajvanlar]
tame (e.g., ~ hamster)	evcil	[ævdʒiʎ]
to tame (vt)	evcilleştirmek	[ævdʒillæʃtirmæk]
to breed (vt)	yetiştirmek	[jætiʃtirmæk]

farm	çiftlik	[tʃiftlik]
poultry	kümse hayvanları	[kymsæ hajvanları]

cattle	çiftlik hayvanları	[tʃiftlik hajvanları]
herd (cattle)	sürü	[syry]

stable	ahır	[ahır]
pigsty	domuz ahırı	[domuz ahırı]
cowshed	inek ahırı	[inæk ahırı]
rabbit hutch	tavşan kafesi	[tavʃan kafæsi]
hen house	tavuk kümesi	[tavuk kymæsi]

90. Birds

bird	kuş	[kuʃ]
pigeon	güvercin	[gyværdʒin]
sparrow	serçe	[særtʃæ]
tit	baştankara	[baʃtaŋkara]
magpie	saksağan	[saksa:n]

raven	kara karga, kuzgun	[kara karga], [kuzgun]
crow	karga	[karga]
jackdaw	küçük karga	[kytʃuk karga]
rook	ekin kargası	[ækin kargası]

duck	ördek	[ørdæk]
goose	kaz	[kaz]
pheasant	sülün	[sylyn]

eagle	kartal	[kartal]
hawk	atmaca	[atmadʒa]
falcon	doğan	[doan]
vulture	akbaba	[akbaba]
condor (Andean ~)	kondor	[kondor]

swan	kuğu	[ku:]
crane	turna	[turna]
stork	leylek	[læjlæk]

parrot	papağan	[papa:n]
hummingbird	sinekkuşu	[sinæk kuʃu]
peacock	tavus	[tavus]

ostrich	deve kuşu	[dævæ kuʃu]
heron	balıkçıl	[balıktʃil]
flamingo	flamingo	[flamiŋo]
pelican	pelikan	[pælikan]

nightingale	bülbül	[byʎbyʎ]
swallow	kırlangıç	[kırlaŋıtʃ]

thrush	ardıç kuşu	[ardıtʃ kuʃu]
song thrush	öter ardıç kuşu	[øtær ardıtʃ kuʃu]
blackbird	karatavuk	[kara tavuk]

swift	sağan	[sa:n]
lark	toygar	[tojgar]
quail	bıldırcın	[bıldırdʒın]

woodpecker	ağaçkakan	[a:tʃkakan]
cuckoo	guguk	[guguk]
owl	baykuş	[bajkuʃ]
eagle owl	puhu kuşu	[puhu kuʃu]

wood grouse	çalıhorozu	[ʧalı horozu]
black grouse	kayın tavuğu	[kajın tavuː]
partridge	keklik	[kæklik]

starling	sığırcık	[sıjırdʒık]
canary	kanarya	[kanarja]
hazel grouse	çil	[ʧiʎ]
chaffinch	ispinoz	[ispinoz]
bullfinch	şakrak kuşu	[ʃakrak kuʃu]

seagull	martı	[martı]
albatross	albatros	[aʎbatros]
penguin	penguen	[pæŋuæn]

91. Fish. Marine animals

bream	çapak balığı	[ʧapak balıː]
carp	sazan	[sazan]
perch	tatlı su levreği	[tatlı su lævræi]
catfish	yayın	[jajın]
pike	turna balığı	[turna balıː]

| salmon | som balığı | [som balıː] |
| sturgeon | mersin balığı | [mærsin balıː] |

herring	ringa	[riŋa]
Atlantic salmon	som, somon	[som], [somon]
mackerel	uskumru	[uskumru]
flatfish	kalkan	[kalkan]

zander, pike perch	uzunlevrek	[uzunlævræk]
cod	morina balığı	[morina balıː]
tuna	ton balığı	[ton balıː]
trout	alabalık	[alabalık]

eel	yılan balığı	[jılan balıː]
electric ray	torpilbalığı	[torpil balıː]
moray eel	murana	[murana]
piranha	pirana	[pirana]

shark	köpek balığı	[køpæk balıː]
dolphin	yunus	[junus]
whale	balina	[balina]

crab	yengeç	[jæŋæʧ]
jellyfish	denizanası	[dæniz anası]
octopus	ahtapot	[ahtapot]

| starfish | deniz yıldızı | [dæniz jıldızı] |
| sea urchin | deniz kirpisi | [dæniz kirpisi] |

seahorse	denizatı	[dænizatı]
oyster	istiridye	[istiridʲæ]
shrimp	karides	[karidæs]
lobster	ıstakoz	[ıstakoz]
spiny lobster	langust	[laŋust]

92. Amphibians. Reptiles

snake	yılan	[jılan]
venomous (snake)	zehirli	[zæhirli]
viper	engerek	[æŋiræk]
cobra	kobra	[kobra]
python	piton	[piton]
boa	boa yılanı	[boa jılanı]
grass snake	çayır yılanı	[tʃajır jılanı]
rattle snake	çıngıraklı yılan	[tʃırgıraklı jılan]
anaconda	anakonda	[anakonda]
lizard	kertenkele	[kærtæŋkælæ]
iguana	iguana	[iguana]
monitor lizard	varan	[varan]
salamander	salamandra	[salamandra]
chameleon	bukalemun	[bukalæmun]
scorpion	akrep	[akræp]
turtle	kaplumbağa	[kaplumba:]
frog	kurbağa	[kurba:]
toad	kara kurbağa	[kara kurba:]
crocodile	timsah	[timsah]

93. Insects

insect, bug	böcek, haşere	[bødʒæk], [haʃæræ]
butterfly	kelebek	[kælæbæk]
ant	karınca	[karındʒa]
fly	sinek	[sinæk]
mosquito	sivri sinek	[sivri sinæk]
beetle	böcek	[bødʒæk]
wasp	eşek arısı	[æʃæk arısı]
bee	arı	[arı]
bumblebee	toprak yabanarısı	[toprak jabanarası]
gadfly	at sineği	[at sinæi]
spider	örümcek	[ørymdʒæk]
spider's web	örümcek ağı	[ørymdʒæk aı]

dragonfly	**kız böceği**	[kız bɵdʒæi]
grasshopper	**çekirge**	[tʃækirgæ]
moth (night butterfly)	**pervane**	[pærvanæ]

cockroach	**hamam böceği**	[hamam bɵdʒæi]
tick	**kene, sakırga**	[kænæ], [sakırga]
flea	**pire**	[piræ]
midge	**tatarcık**	[tatardʒık]

locust	**çekirge**	[tʃækirgæ]
snail	**sümüklü böcek**	[symykly bɵdʒæk]
cricket	**cırcırböceği**	[dʒırdʒır bɵdʒæi]
lightning bug	**ateş böceği**	[atæʃ bɵdʒæi]
ladybug	**uğur böceği**	[u:r bɵdʒæi]
cockchafer	**mayıs böceği**	[majıs bɵdʒæi]

leech	**sülük**	[sylyk]
caterpillar	**tırtıl**	[tırtıl]
earthworm	**solucan**	[soludʒan]
larva	**kurtçuk**	[kurtʃuk]

FLORA

94. Trees

tree	ağaç	[aːtʃ]
deciduous (adj)	geniş yapraklı	[gæniʃ japraklı]
coniferous (adj)	iğne yapraklı	[iːnæ japraklı]
evergreen (adj)	her dem taze	[hær dæm tazæ]
apple tree	elma ağacı	[æʎma aːdʒı]
pear tree	armut ağacı	[armut aːdʒı]
sweet cherry tree	kiraz ağacı	[kiraz aːdʒı]
sour cherry tree	vişne ağacı	[viʃnæ aːdʒı]
plum tree	erik ağacı	[ærik aːdʒı]
birch	huş ağacı	[huʃ aːdʒı]
oak	meşe	[mæʃæ]
linden tree	ıhlamur	[ıhlamur]
aspen	titrek kavak	[titræk kavak]
maple	akça ağaç	[aktʃa aːtʃ]
spruce	ladin ağacı	[ladin aːdʒı]
pine	çam ağacı	[tʃam aːdʒı]
larch	melez ağacı	[mælæz aːdʒı]
fir tree	köknar	[køknar]
cedar	sedir	[sædir]
poplar	kavak	[kavak]
rowan	üvez ağacı	[juvæz aːdʒı]
willow	söğüt	[søjut]
alder	kızılağaç	[kızılaːtʃ]
beech	kayın	[kajın]
elm	karaağaç	[kara aːtʃ]
ash (tree)	dişbudak ağacı	[diʃbudak aːdʒı]
chestnut	kestane	[kæstanæ]
magnolia	manolya	[manoʎja]
palm tree	palmiye	[paʎmijæ]
cypress	servi	[særvi]
baobab	baobab ağacı	[baobab aːdʒı]
eucalyptus	okaliptüs	[okaliptys]
sequoia	sekoya	[sækoja]

95. Shrubs

bush	çalı	[ʧalı]
shrub	çalılık	[ʧalılık]
grapevine	üzüm	[juzym]
vineyard	bağ	[ba:]
raspberry bush	ahududu	[ahududu]
redcurrant bush	kırmızı frenk üzümü	[kırmızı fræŋk juzymy]
gooseberry bush	bektaşi üzümü	[bæktaʃi juzymy]
acacia	akasya	[akasja]
barberry	diken üzümü	[dikæn juzymy]
jasmine	yasemin	[jasæmin]
juniper	ardıç	[ardıʧ]
rosebush	gül ağacı	[gyʎ a:dʒı]
dog rose	yaban gülü	[jaban gyly]

96. Fruits. Berries

fruit	meyve	[mæjvæ]
fruits	meyveler	[mæjvælær]
apple	elma	[æʎma]
pear	armut	[armut]
plum	erik	[ærik]
strawberry	çilek	[ʧilæk]
sour cherry	vişne	[viʃnæ]
sweet cherry	kiraz	[kiraz]
grape	üzüm	[juzym]
raspberry	ahududu	[ahududu]
blackcurrant	siyah frenküzümü	[sijah fræŋkjuzymy]
redcurrant	kırmızı frenk üzümü	[kırmızı fræŋk juzymy]
gooseberry	bektaşi üzümü	[bæktaʃi juzymy]
cranberry	kızılcık	[kızıldʒık]
orange	portakal	[portakal]
mandarin	mandalina	[mandalina]
pineapple	ananas	[ananas]
banana	muz	[muz]
date	hurma	[hurma]
lemon	limon	[limon]
apricot	kayısı	[kajısı]
peach	şeftali	[ʃæftali]
kiwi	kivi	[kivi]

grapefruit	greypfrut	[græjpfrut]
berry	meyve, yemiş	[mæjvæ], [jæmiʃ]
berries	yemişler	[jæmiʃler]
cowberry	kırmızı yabanmersini	[kırmızı jaban mærsini]
field strawberry	yabani çilek	[jabani tʃilæk]
bilberry	yaban mersini	[jaban mærsini]

97. Flowers. Plants

| flower | çiçek | [tʃitʃæk] |
| bouquet (of flowers) | demet | [dæmæt] |

rose (flower)	gül	[gyʎ]
tulip	lale	[ʎalæ]
carnation	karanfil	[karanfiʎ]
gladiolus	glayöl	[glajoʎ]

cornflower	peygamber çiçeği	[pæjgambær tʃitʃæi]
bluebell	çançiçeği	[tʃantʃitʃæi]
dandelion	hindiba	[hindiba]
camomile	papatya	[papatja]

aloe	sarısabır	[sarısabır]
cactus	kaktüs	[kaktys]
rubber plant, ficus	kauçuk ağacı	[kautʃuk a:dʒı]

lily	zambak	[zambak]
geranium	sardunya	[sardunija]
hyacinth	sümbül	[symbyʎ]

mimosa	mimoza	[mimoza]
narcissus	nergis	[nærgis]
nasturtium	latinçiçeği	[latin tʃitʃæi]

orchid	orkide	[orkidæ]
peony	şakayık	[ʃakajık]
violet	menekşe	[mænækʃæ]

pansy	hercai menekşe	[hærdʒai mænækʃæ]
forget-me-not	unutmabeni	[unutmabæni]
daisy	papatya	[papatja]

poppy	haşhaş	[haʃhaʃ]
hemp	kendir	[kændir]
mint	nane	[nanæ]

lily of the valley	inci çiçeği	[indʒi tʃitʃæi]
snowdrop	kardelen	[kardælæn]
nettle	ısırgan otu	[ısırgan otu]
sorrel	kuzukulağı	[kuzukulaı]

water lily	**beyaz nilüfer**	[bæjaz nilyfær]
fern	**eğreltiotu**	[ægræltiotu]
lichen	**liken**	[likæn]
tropical greenhouse	**limonluk**	[limonlyk]
grass lawn	**çimen**	[ʧimæn]
flowerbed	**çiçek tarhı**	[ʧiʧæk tarhı]
plant	**bitki**	[bitki]
grass, herb	**ot**	[ot]
blade of grass	**ot çöpü**	[ot ʧopy]
leaf	**yaprak**	[japrak]
petal	**taçyaprağı**	[tatʃjapraı]
stem	**sap**	[sap]
tuber	**yumru**	[jumru]
young plant (shoot)	**filiz**	[filiz]
thorn	**diken**	[dikæn]
to blossom (vi)	**çiçeklenmek**	[ʧiʧæklænmæk]
to fade, to wither	**solmak**	[solmak]
smell (odor)	**koku**	[koku]
to cut (flowers)	**kesmek**	[kæsmæk]
to pick (a flower)	**koparmak**	[koparmak]

98. Cereals, grains

grain	**tahıl, tane**	[tahıl], [tanæ]
cereal crops	**tahıllar**	[tahıllar]
ear (of barley, etc.)	**başak**	[baʃak]
wheat	**buğday**	[bu:daj]
rye	**çavdar**	[ʧavdar]
oats	**yulaf**	[julaf]
millet	**darı**	[darı]
barley	**arpa**	[arpa]
corn	**mısır**	[mısır]
rice	**pirinç**	[pirinʧ]
buckwheat	**karabuğday**	[karabu:daj]
pea plant	**bezelye**	[bæzæʎʲæ]
kidney bean	**fasulye**	[fasuʎʲæ]
soy	**soya**	[soja]
lentil	**mercimek**	[mærdʒimæk]
beans (pulse crops)	**bakla**	[bakla]

COUNTRIES OF THE WORLD

99. Countries. Part 1

Afghanistan	Afganistan	[afganistan]
Albania	Arnavutluk	[arnavutluk]
Argentina	Arjantin	[arʒantin]
Armenia	Ermenistan	[ærmænistan]
Australia	Avustralya	[avustraʎja]
Austria	Avusturya	[avusturja]
Azerbaijan	Azerbaycan	[azærbajdʒan]

The Bahamas	Bahama adaları	[bahama adaları]
Bangladesh	Bangladeş	[baŋladæʃ]
Belarus	Beyaz Rusya	[bæjaz rusja]
Belgium	Belçika	[bæʎtʃika]
Bolivia	Bolivya	[bolivja]
Bosnia-Herzegovina	Bosna-Hersek	[bosna hærtsæk]
Brazil	Brezilya	[bræziʎja]
Bulgaria	Bulgaristan	[bulgaristan]

Cambodia	Kamboçya	[kambotʃja]
Canada	Kanada	[kanada]
Chile	Şili	[ʃili]
China	Çin	[tʃin]
Colombia	Kolombiya	[kolombija]
Croatia	Hırvatistan	[hırvatistan]
Cuba	Küba	[kyba]
Cyprus	Kıbrıs	[kıbrıs]
Czech Republic	Çek Cumhuriyeti	[tʃæk dʒumhurijæti]

Denmark	Danimarka	[danimarka]
Dominican Republic	Dominik Cumhuriyeti	[dominik dʒumhurijæti]
Ecuador	Ekvator	[ækvator]
Egypt	Mısır	[mısır]
England	İngiltere	[iŋiʎtæræ]
Estonia	Estonya	[æstoŋja]
Finland	Finlandiya	[finʎandja]
France	Fransa	[fransa]
French Polynesia	Fransız Polinezisi	[fransız polinæzisi]

Georgia	Gürcistan	[gyrdʒistan]
Germany	Almanya	[almaŋja]
Ghana	Gana	[gana]
Great Britain	Büyük Britanya	[byjuk britaŋja]
Greece	Yunanistan	[junanistan]

| Haiti | Haiti | [haiti] |
| Hungary | Macaristan | [madʒaristan] |

100. Countries. Part 2

Iceland	İzlanda	[izlanda]
India	Hindistan	[hindistan]
Indonesia	Endonezya	[ændonæzja]
Iran	İran	[iran]
Iraq	Irak	[ırak]
Ireland	İrlanda	[irlanda]
Israel	İsrail	[israiʎ]
Italy	İtalya	[itaʎja]

Jamaica	Jamaika	[ʒamajka]
Japan	Japonya	[ʒapoɲja]
Jordan	Ürdün	[urdyn]
Kazakhstan	Kazakistan	[kazakistan]
Kenya	Kenya	[kæɲja]
Kirghizia	Kırgızistan	[kırgızistan]
Kuwait	Kuveyt	[kuvæjt]

Laos	Laos	[laos]
Latvia	Letonya	[lætoɲja]
Lebanon	Lübnan	[lybnan]
Libya	Libya	[libja]
Liechtenstein	Lihtenştayn	[lihtænʃtajn]
Lithuania	Litvanya	[litvaɲja]
Luxembourg	Lüksemburg	[lyksæmburg]

Macedonia	Makedonya	[makædoɲja]
Madagascar	Madagaskar	[madagaskar]
Malaysia	Malezya	[malæzja]
Malta	Malta	[maʎta]
Mexico	Meksika	[mæksika]
Moldavia	Moldova	[moldova]

Monaco	Monako	[monako]
Mongolia	Moğolistan	[moːlistan]
Montenegro	Karadağ	[karadaː]

| Morocco | Fas | [fas] |
| Myanmar | Myanmar | [mjanmar] |

Namibia	Namibya	[namibja]
Nepal	Nepal	[næpal]
Netherlands	Hollanda	[hollanda]
New Zealand	Yeni Zelanda	[jæni zælanda]
North Korea	Kuzey Kore	[kuzæj koræ]
Norway	Norveç	[norvætʃ]

101. Countries. Part 3

Pakistan	**Pakistan**	[pakistan]
Panama	**Panama**	[panama]
Paraguay	**Paraguay**	[paraguaj]
Peru	**Peru**	[pæru]
Poland	**Polonya**	[poloɲja]
Portugal	**Portekiz**	[portækiz]
Romania	**Romanya**	[romaɲja]
Russia	**Rusya**	[rusja]
Saudi Arabia	**Suudi Arabistan**	[su:di arabistan]
Scotland	**İskoçya**	[iskotʃja]
Senegal	**Senegal**	[sænægal]
Serbia	**Sırbistan**	[sırbistan]
Slovakia	**Slovakya**	[slovakja]
Slovenia	**Slovenya**	[slovæɲja]
South Africa	**Güney Afrika Cumhuriyeti**	[gynæj afrika dʒumhurijæti]
South Korea	**Güney Kore**	[gynæj koræ]
Spain	**İspanya**	[ispaɲja]
Suriname	**Surinam**	[surinam]
Sweden	**İsveç**	[isvætʃ]
Switzerland	**İsviçre**	[isvitʃræ]
Syria	**Suriye**	[surijæ]
Taiwan	**Tayvan**	[tajvan]
Tajikistan	**Tacikistan**	[tadʒikistan]
Tanzania	**Tanzanya**	[tanzaɲja]
Tasmania	**Tazmanya**	[tazmanija]
Thailand	**Tayland**	[tailand]
Tunisia	**Tunus**	[tunus]
Turkey	**Türkiye**	[tyrkijæ]
Turkmenistan	**Türkmenistan**	[tyrkmænistan]
Ukraine	**Ukrayna**	[ukrajna]
United Arab Emirates	**Birleşik Arap Emirlikleri**	[birlæʃik arap æmirliklæri]
United States of America	**Amerika Birleşik Devletleri**	[amærika birlæʃik dævlætlæri]
Uruguay	**Uruguay**	[urugvaj]
Uzbekistan	**Özbekistan**	[øzbækistan]
Vatican	**Vatikan**	[vatikan]
Venezuela	**Venezuela**	[vænæzuæla]
Vietnam	**Vietnam**	[vɪætnam]
Zanzibar	**Zanzibar**	[zanzibar]